CARVING
THE UNUSUAL

E.J. TANGERMAN

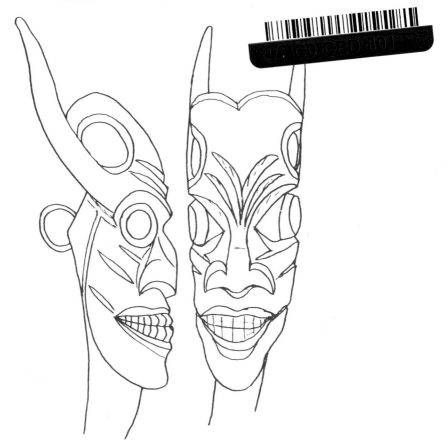

![Sterling logo] Sterling Publishing Co., Inc. New York

Other books by E. J. Tangerman

Capturing Personality in Woodcarving
Carving Faces and Figures in Wood
Carving Flora and Fables in Wood
Carving Religious Motifs in Wood
Carving Wooden Animals
Relief Woodcarving

Library of Congress Cataloging in Publication Data

Tangerman, E.J. (Elmer John), 1907–
    Carving the unusual.

    (Home craftsman series)
    Includes index.
    1. Wood-carving.   I. Title.   II. Series.
TT199.7.T344 1982   736'.4   82-50544

Contents

Fig. 1. A Jamaican lad sits at Folly Plantation and carves, with three carpenter's chisels and a whittled mallet. The figure is of a woman going to market, wearing hat and billowing dress. His reason for carving: "I can sell it to somebody like you!"

Why Carve the Unusual?

IN KOWLOON ONE DAY, I ASKED A SALESMAN in a carved-ivory shop what *he* carved. "Elephants," he said. "Horses are selling better," I offered. "Have you ever tried to carve one?" He shook his head. "No," he replied, "I only carve elephants." Indeed, there are whittlers who make only old boots or wooden chains, and carvers who make only decoys, signs or furniture with traditional motifs. I've met professional cabinetmakers who never tried carving at all until they retired.

This book is not for any of the above. It is an effort to assemble a number of unusual ideas in materials, subject, technique and treatment that I have found refreshing alternatives to typical woodcarving and predetermined commissions. The chapters are arranged by difficulty; materials other than wood occupy their own chapters toward the back in most instances. Included are chapters on wood, tools, sharpening and changing pattern size. Finish is indicated piece-by-piece, and I have also provided traceable patterns for a number of them. Because these carvings are unusual, I have already sold some, and could have sold more.

Many of the designs are not American, because some of the most unusual of carvings are foreign in origin. Most are, however, folk art rather than formal art, because the latter usually follows traditional patterns available from many sources and mostly utilitarian in application. These designs are largely for fun and "for a change." Go to it!

E. J. Tangerman

CHAPTER I

The Woods to Carve

(If it is wood you're carving)

THE COMMONEST WOODS FOR WHITTLING in the United States are basswood and white pine, in that order, followed by a recent import from Indochina called jelutong. All are very light in color, soft, readily carved and sanded, and are colored with oils, acrylics or stains. They do tend to split (particularly the pine), wear, crumble and discolor with time, and they won't hold detail. None has a visible figure or grain marking of any value.

Slightly harder are butternut and, quite recently, paulownia, which are light tan with darker grain. Then there's cedar, which may crumble and cause color problems. Still harder are the fruit and nut woods such as pecan, cherry, apple and, occasionally, plum and pear. These will hold detail reasonably well, and are hard, but are subject to warping, checking and insect attack. All will take even the glossiest stain and finishes, and should not be painted, except in special circumstances—and then, tinted. Then there are red alder, myrtle, redwood (soft and hard streaks), tupelo, and catalpa. They are difficult to whittle, and work better with chisels and a mallet. Still harder are black walnut, maple, holly and oak. Of these, walnut is the best wood to carve and finish, though it does tend to finish quite dark, and must be well-lit for detail to show. Maple is hard, but relatively light in color, long-lasting and strong. Oak in the United States tends to be open-grained and coarse, but strong, and the figure or grain looks good when finished. Also, it is a medium brown and works well for statuary and panels that are to be finished in natural color. Holly, one of the whitest woods, is very dense-grained and usually available only in small pieces, but holds detail extremely well.

There are dozens of other American woods such as the very hard mesquite, osage orange and ironwood of the American southwest, magnolia, mimosa, cypress and ash in the southeast, willow, elm and so on, but these are not for beginners or normal carving. They tend to cause problems, and should be used primarily for particular qualities.

One of the best-known woods is mahogany, which is really a very general term for a whole family of woods (and is often applied to woods that aren't really mahoganies at all). There is prima vera, which is often called "white mahogany" because it can be stained to be indistiguishable; I have three or four occasional tables made from it. Then there is luanda, or luan, which resembles mahogany, but isn't. Generally, the best mahoganies are those from Central America. Most Philippine and African mahogany is inferior and given to splitting, as well as being open-grained.

My favorite wood is still teak from Thailand and Burma. There are Chinese, African and Latin-American teaks, but they are coarser in grain. Teak is immune to insects, unlikely to warp, rot, or check, will stand any weather (it is used for ship decks), and can be kept finished with occasional applications of oil. It does not change dimension with humidity to any degree, which makes it ideal for outdoor carvings. It is about as hard as walnut, but lighter in color.

Another attractive wood is rosewood, which also comes from many Latin-American countries as well as Africa. It varies widely in color from rosy red to brown; I have a Mexican piece that includes suggestions of purple and green. It is hard, but not as hard as cocobola or lignum vitae. These woods are very expensive, and should not be used for casual carvings. Most of the African woods such as beef, thuya, bubinga, and zebra tend to split and are hard to carve. This is also true of purpleheart and greenheart from South America, though they provide unique colors difficult to find elsewhere. Another wood of this type is vermilion, which is hard, close-grained, and finishes to a rich red; these last three woods are excellent for pendants.

Most expensive and rarest of woods is pink ivory, which is delicate pinkish-white to light red in color and interesting to work. There are dozens of other woods, some with elaborate figure. Lime, pear and harewood (English sycamore) are imported from Europe for special uses. For most carvers, however, it is best to carve what is available, at least for starters. Exotic woods should be saved for exotic ideas.

CHAPTER II

First, Something about Tools...

ANCIENT MAN CARVED THE MATERIALS HE HAD with whatever tools he could devise. His incentives were undoubtedly to placate the gods or worship them, to make a tool easier to hold and to make an image for himself or his children. Wood was abundant in most areas and could be cut by stone, so the stone knife and chisel found early use, followed by the axe and the adz when someone discovered how to make and bind on a handle. The point is, ancient man got along with relatively few tools. So can you, until you know what you need.

The most universal tool is the knife, particularly the pocketknife, because it is so portable and adaptable. A good one can cut a wide variety of materials, certainly any mentioned in this book. Because man is so inventive, he has developed an extraordinary number of variations on the knife, each with its own special purpose and advantages. You can buy any number of blade and handle shapes, even blades with blank handles you can carve to fit your hand. But it is better to start with a good pocketknife, with a maximum of two or three carbon-steel blades (stainless won't hold an edge as well) and no belt clips, can openers or corkscrews to chafe your palm. Because the knife will change position in your hand for various cuts, it should have an essentially smooth and uniform handle, comfortable to grip. Blades should include at least one with a saber point, usually the big one—known as a B-clip. The other one or two should be pen, spear or an equivalent. Be sure blades open and close easily, yet do not wobble, and open out straight and firmly.

If you find carving a particular material or subject preferable, you can branch out and get specially shaped fixed-blade knives to suit what you're doing. These are easier and safer to use at home—the blade won't snap shut on your finger—but they aren't as portable. However, I know tool enthusiasts who have made their own knives from old saw-blades or straight razors and have special cases to carry them in, just as I carry a roll with a number of chisels. Mine includes sharpening aides, and so should yours. Have at least one narrow and thin blade to get into concavities and tight corners, and one wide, heavy blade for roughing. I also find that a blade with a concave cutting edge (which I call a hook), originally developed for leatherworking, is helpful in carving details. Blades should be short—not over 1½ in (3.8 cm) long for most work—kept sharp, and oiled to avoid rust.

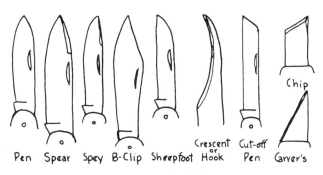

Fig. 2. Knife blades.

Many sources are eager to sell you a *set* of carving tools, a mixture of types supposedly put together by an "expert" that includes some you may never use, as was the case with the 9-tool set I bought originally. Further, you don't have to buy the finest tools available; buy cheap ones until you find out what you really need, then supplement with better quality. With a little care, you'll find that cheap tools work almost as well as expensive ones. They do for me.

Woodcarving tools have a long history and, thus, a vocabulary all their own. The straight chisel, like a carpenter's chisel but lighter, is called a *firmer*. It is sharpened from both sides so it doesn't dig in. If the edge is at an angle to the blade length it is called a *skew*, and is used for getting into corners, much as a knife would be (I use the knife). The rounded chisels are called *gouges*, as in carpentry, but come in a wide range of widths and curvatures or *sweeps* from almost flat to U-shaped. The very U-shaped ones are called *fluters*, particularly in small sizes. One of the most useful of gouges is a very small half-round one called a *veiner*, because it's used to carve veins, hair and any other very small grooves. Its alternate is the *V-tool* (or parting tool, from wood-turning), also used for grooving. This is essentially two firmers put together in a vee; it is difficult to sharpen because of this, but it cuts two sides at once. There are also more specialized tools such as the

9

macaroni, which cuts a 3-sided groove with a flat bottom and square corners, and a *fluteroni*, which cuts a similar groove with rounded corners. These are very difficult to sharpen and of almost no use to amateur carvers.

Carving tools may have several kinds of handles, depending upon their size and source. In the Orient, tools are long and thin and often without handles. Smaller tools can be bought with palm-grip handles such as an engraver has on a burin. I find these of little use except for details on hand-held work. Conventional handles are straight, round, hex or octagonal, and are made of various woods depending upon country of origin. Many are now maple or birch, and some are plastic. I prefer wooden hex handles because I use a mallet most of the time and wood takes the blows better, while the hex lets me adjust the tool easily and prevents rolling when it is put down. You can even make your own handles, with bits of pipe for collars.

The rear of a chisel ends in a tang, a pointed end that goes into a hole in the handle as far as its collar will allow, while a ring on the handle prevents it from splitting under the wedging action of the tang. Obviously, larger chisels must have tapered shanks to end in a tang, which leads to the spade or *fishtail* design (Fig. 3) where the blade is wider than the shank. This is also done on many smaller tools because it gives greater clearance in carving and lightens the tool. Also, because straight tools are of limited use when entering certain areas, tools are made with bent shanks, ranging from a very short and half-circular bend called a *knuckle*, through a short bend (*spoon*) and on to a long bend. Some tools are made with similar bends backward, and are called *back-bent* tools, but are of lesser value. There are also *dog-leg* tools, in which a double bend offsets the cutting edge from the line of the shank.

Carving tools may be driven by the hands alone on small work in soft woods. On hand-held work, the palm tools are easy because they require only one hand. But they are very slow in material removal (as is a pocketknife), though they work well on ivory and bone. If the piece can be held or secured in any way, the long-handled tools are preferable, since one hand can supply push while the other guides and restrains the tool. The method I use is to hold the chisel in one hand and drive it with a mallet of suitable weight for the work being done. This way, I get more precise control of the cut with less danger of splitting—a problem with hand pushing because it is difficult to control arm-muscle force accurately.

Mallets can be designed to your specifications, or bought ready-made. I prefer the traditional potato-masher type, and in recent years have used those with plastic or rubber faces to reduce shock in my arthritic shoulders. Other carvers prefer babbitt-faced mallets or even copper or brass ones, but these tend to split tool handles, as an ordinary hammer would. Further, their diameter is small, so more attention must be paid to hitting the handle end squarely.

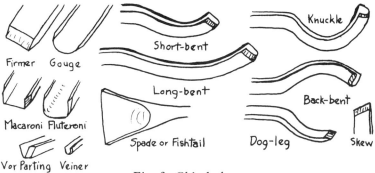

Fig. 3. Chisel shapes.

In addition to these specialized carving tools, there are also a great number of auxiliary tools used by specialty carvers. These include various kinds of saws, such as saber and scroll saws, rasps of various sizes (much-used for decoy carving in soft woods), riffler files in various shapes to smooth tight corners, scrapers, hand routers and the usual carpenter's tools, including planes and chisels. Carpenter's chisels, incidentally, are cheaper and heavier than equivalent woodcarving tools and, thus, good for roughing. The hand axe, shingling hatchet and adz are also used, particularly on larger and rougher work like wooden Indians and totem poles. Indians of the American northwest coast, Africans and Italians use adzes for most carving.

Americans who are accustomed to mechanizing everything have added a whole series of power tools to this list, including chain saws, bandsaws, circular saws, sanders of various types—including hand-held ones that take cutters or burrs as well as grinding shapes—and even pneumatic or electric hammers. With power tools, there is always increased danger, and with some it is advisable to wear goggles and mask, and to work in an area where noise, dust and possible vapors (from such woods as cocobola or rosewood) will not affect others. These power tools remind me too much of mass production, so I shy away from using them unless I have a large block with a great deal of roughing to be done or a piece in which the contour permits me to cut out and save a smaller section. Rotary tools tend to chew the wood away, and small burrs tend to burn the surface.

For conventional amateur work, particularly with chisels, you may want to have some form of holding device. I have used a machinist's vise, opening about 4½ in (11 cm), for years, and a long-leg carpenter's vise for larger pieces. In recent years, I have also used the carver's screw—which screws through a bench or table into the base of the workpiece and holds it with a tightened wingnut. Mine are hand-made by a friend from lag bolts or threaded steel rod. If the piece is relatively large, no clamping will be necessary as its own weight will hold it. Panels can be held by nailing through scrap areas, by holding with a benchplate (a square of plywood with a stop-board), or just placing them on a section of discarded ribbed-rubber doormat. You can, of course, have a carver's bench, a 4-legged stand or even a stand of the type sketched in figure 4, but they take up room and begin to require a shop or studio. I do most of my carving seated next to the fireplace in my living room, with the work on my knees or lying on a bridge table. When clamping is needed, I adjourn to my cellar workbench or to a picnic table on the terrace, both of which can take clamps, vises or carver's screws, as well as any amount of shock from mallet blows.

Carving tools, by the way, are sized by the width of the cutting edge, in inches from ¹⁄₁₆ in (1.6 mm) to ⅜ in (9.5 mm) in sixteenths, on up to 1 in (25.4 mm) in eighths, and in larger steps to the maximum, usually about 2½ in (6.4 cm) for flat gouges. European tools are sized in millimeters: 1, 2, 3, 4, 5, 6, 7, 8, 10, 12, 16, 20, 25, 30, 35 and so on (1 mm = 0.039 in). Gouges are usually numbered also by the "London" system that measures arc or radius of the sweep. A firmer is No. 1, a skew No. 2, a flat gouge No. 3 and a U-shaped one No. 11 or 12, with the other arcs in between. Some suppliers use other numbers for the special tools, from this series or their own catalogue numbers. Charles M. Sayers, who taught panel carving, suggested four tools with which to start: ½-in (13-mm), or ⅜- to ⅝-in (9.5- to 16-mm); ⅝-in (16-mm) No. 5 straight gouge; 1-in (25.4-mm) No. 3, or ⅞-in (22-mm) straight gouge, and a ⅜-in (9.5-mm) No. 7 straight gouge. For relief carving, he added a ⅜-in (9.5-mm) No. 5 straight gouge. H. M. Sutter, who has taught panel carving for over 30 years, starts his students—often teachers themselves—with five tools: ⅜-in (9.5-mm) No. 3 and ⅝-in (16-mm) No. 5 straight gouges (these two preferably fishtail); ⅜-in (9.5-mm) No. 9 straight gouge; ¹⁄₃₂-in (.79-mm) No. 11 veiner and a ⅜-in (9.5-mm) No. 41 parting or V-tool, plus an all-purpose carver's knife.

Note that neither suggests fancy shapes or skew chisels, at least to start. Begin small, then buy with the guidance of an experienced carver—or you're likely to end up with heavy patternmakers' chisels or worse.

To carve the harder materials included in this book, try small chisels, particularly the veiner and V-tool. I find engraver's burins (solid chisels) of little help, though palm tools can work well. Riffler files will help on occasion, as will power grinders; Eskimo and German ivory carvers are both using these now. Also of help will be a chamois-skin or leather pillow filled with sand. The work can be nestled in it with less danger of rolling and slipping. Further, most of the hard materials are difficult to hold in a vise or clamp because they are rounded in shape and brittle.

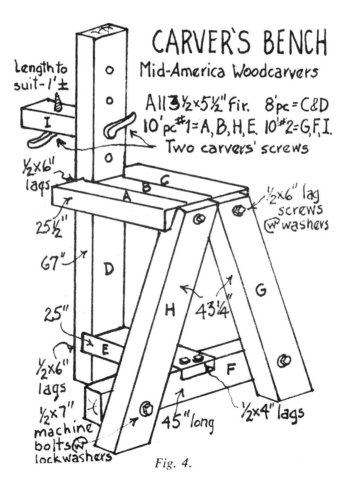

Fig. 4.

CHAPTER III

Fun with Animals

Caricature and stylizing from various countries
show a broad range of treatments

THE BASIC RULE OF CARICATURE, as opposed to crudity, is that the designer emphasizes—subtly—true characteristics and peculiarities of a particular subject. It is much the same with stylizing; you formalize and simplify the distinguishing characteristics without destroying the overall semblance of the original. Stylizing, however, stresses general shape and form at the expense of detail, while caricature highlights notable features of a given subject and, thus, *adds* detail. In either case, you must be familiar with the subject. Lengthening the long neck of a giraffe is not enough; the head and stance must be a giraffe's as well. A pig's snout and tail must be accompanied by the stocky body and some suggestion of a difference in attitude from that of a giraffe.

These figures come from many places and are done in many different ways. Some are from Latin America, where life is still comparatively simple, where the carver is still quite familiar with nature and unaffected by the artificiality and sophistication that warps our sense of humor. Some are meticulously detailed, such as the rosewood armadillo in figure 5, while others, like the alpaca in figure 7, are virtually stripped of it. The heraldic lion from Peru (Fig. 9) still retains a great deal of realism, though the shapes have been simplified and formalized. By comparison, T. E. Haag's *Cat and the Fiddle* and *Adder and Eve* retain only the barest suggestion of the original subject—but it is there nevertheless.

The owl and cat caricatures in figures 13 and 14 have painted-on comic features. The other animals in figure 14, all from Argentina, also have painted eyes and pupils—black for a male, red for a female—and a silhouette effect enhanced by using a thicker block for the body. The cat even has the suggestion of a smile—a smile, but not a horse laugh. Remember: Something must be left to the observer's imagination, something that will repay his observation by stirring an emotion (usually humor). The stirring should not be done with a club, as is so often the case.

Bull and fawn (Figs. 17 and 18), from Spain, show excellent stylizing. The bull breathes power, the fawn airiness. Both rely on simple sawn silhouettes to convey their characteristics; the bull is thick, with horns ready, while the fawn is carved thin and leaping. Very little shaping has been done on the fawn, and none on the bull. And both abandon rigid reliance on wood. You'll notice that the fawn's tail is a bit of rough cord, frayed, and that the bull has inserted silver-strip horns and tail. Now compare these to the penguin in figure 15, which uses sharp contrast for its effectiveness. The simple form is painted to simulate the darker feathers; again, there is no detailing, not even an eye.

With a little experience and effort, you can do your own stylized carvings and have fun at them. The primary requirement is to study your subject to find out what is different or dominant about it, and then to combine those elements in a pleasing design—with smooth, long curves and lines. The little variations are eliminated, and geometric shapes can then be substituted.

The Seri-Indian-carved birds and fish in ironwood are unusual and compelling because they are readily identifiable. The shapes are realistic, but only a minimum of detail is included so that form and the beauty of the polished wood become most important. The Seri alligator (Fig. 22), on the other hand, is an example of over-detailing. True, its shape alone suggests and defines it, but the carver has added what I feel to be unnecessary detail in teeth, toes and ridged back. But this can sometimes be a matter of opinion and custom.

What is considered over-detailing in one country is often the essence of stylizing in another. Americans think of 30 to 50 percent of a surface as enough carving, the Italians go to 80 percent or thereabouts, and the East Indians go to 100 percent. Consider the Japanese temple carvings in figures 24 and 25. They are 200 years old and include fanciful as well as real animals. They are very definitely stylized, particularly in the fantastic waves and ground growth, but also include much more detail than anyone would use nowadays, even the Japanese. It is hard to avoid over-detailing—take it from an ex-engineer!

Figs. 5–6 (above and below). Stylized armadillo, from Mexico. Tail is inserted, as is typical.

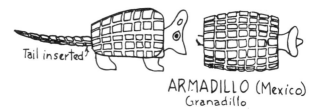

Tail inserted

ARMADILLO (Mexico)
Granadillo

Fig. 7 (right). Three pieces in soft stone, the alpaca (left) and llama in soapstone — from Chile — and the pony in red feldspar (Brazil). All three are polished; none has rough or hard edges.

16

Fig. 8 (above). Four stylized llamas. At left is a Peruvian design that is fairly realistic, at far right a stone one that is thin and stylized. The Peruvian belled llama (second from left) is quite different from the Bolivian one next to it, but both are stockier than the others.

Fig. 9 (left). Heraldic lion by Domingo Fernandez Rimachi, self-taught Indian carver of Cuzco, Peru. Wood is cedar, and the piece is about 18 in (46 cm) tall, a decorative boss. Note that the mane is elaborately detailed although stylized, and that six front-leg claws are shown instead of eight.

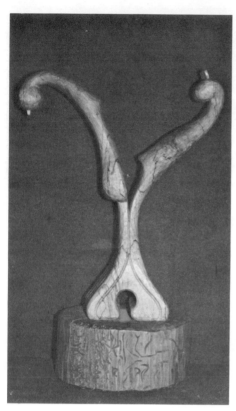

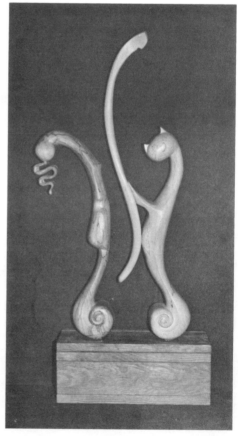

Figs. 10–11 (above and right).
Adder and Eve *and* Cat and the
Fiddle, *by T. E. Haag, Tualatin,
Oregon. Though extremely stylized, subjects are still identifiable
because basic elements such as
bosom and bottom, fiddle-string
ends and ears are emphasized.*

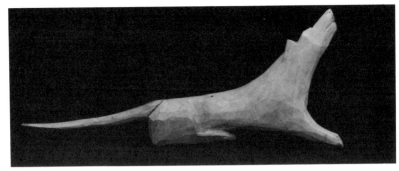

Fig. 12 (above). Hound in copal, by Adrian Xuana Luis of San Martin Tilcajete, Mexico. This primitive carving, by a self-taught Indian, shows surprising strength and imagination. The hound's tail is simply tacked in place.

Fig. 13 (left). Owl from Guerrero is in strongly grained granadillo, and has inserted beak and double-insert eyes that characterize pieces from this area. "Ears" have drilled holes and the claws are delineated, though feathers are not even suggested. Fig. 14 (below). Three Argentinian animal caricatures have the same painted-in eyes, the cat's with blue lids! They are assembled sawed pieces, but could readily be modelled.

STYLIZED
PENGUIN
T.E. Haag US
Maple

Black

Figs. 15–16 (above, left to right).
Penguin by Ted Haag is a simple
form, with no detailing except the
black painting to simulate the
darker feathering. It is 4 in (10
cm) high.

Fig. 17 (above). Stylized bull
from Spain is in a dark, grainy
wood. It is 6½ in (17 cm) long
overall, with inserted silver horns
and flat tail. There is no detailing. Fig. 18 (left). Spanish fawn
is in olive wood, so grain is very
prominent. It is quite stylized,
but very whimsical, having a bit
of cord for a tail and prominent
downcast eyes.

Figs. 19–20 (above and below). Two spreadwing birds in ironwood have only the same general shape. One includes a suggestion of feathering and a streamlined body, while the other has neither. Each is planned to rest on a central-body pivot.

Fig. 21 (right). Dolphin and sailfish, 10 in and 13 in (25 and 33 cm), show emphasis on general shape and on fins. Both have rough-finished bases and are one-piece sculptures in ironwood.

Fig. 22. This alligator, about 18 in (46 cm) long, has been over-detailed. The feet are overly large and show toes, and the back is subdivided, when simple undulation would have suggested the ridging. Also, the snout is poorly shaped and shows teeth, which is unnecessary. It was carved by Seri Indians near Tiburon Island in the Gulf of Mexico, and is a relatively recent and unschooled development in their carving, which previously was limited to simple utilitarian objects.

Fig. 23. A 12-in (30-cm) sailfish in ironwood emphasizes the dorsal fin, which shows ribbing.

Figs. 24–25 (above and below). Extremely elaborate stylizing is evident in these two sections of temple carving in Honso, Akita, Japan. Done about 200 years ago, it includes dragons in stylized waves and a tortoise amid mushrooms and reeds, all originally tinted. Photographs are by Donald P. Berger, an American teaching in Tokyo.

CHAPTER IV
Stylizing Humans

Much variety is possible in technique and purpose

STYLIZING THE HUMAN FIGURE CAN TAKE MANY FORMS beyond the shift from realism to some single or "accepted" treatment that the word may seem to suggest. Thus a stylized figure can become symbolic, near-abstract or so formalized that the connection with the human figure is almost indiscernible. Compare the three figures by T. E. Haag, for example. The low-relief panel of the running girl (Fig. 26) is almost realistic, except for omission of detail in face and feet, while the standing figure (Fig. 27) is recognizable only by the lines of hair and buttocks in a general human outline. Figure 28 has a human face and general, blocky human shape, but otherwise is a geometric design.

Among the Yugoslavian designs there is a similarly wide range, from the almost representational in *Newlyweds* (except for a few exaggerated, stressed elements) to the highly stylized *Measuring*, in which symbolism is very strong. Deliberate duplication is sought in *All the Same* (Fig. 31), while a more developed blockiness is used in the American panel by T. E. Haag (Fig. 26) to obtain a flowing and pleasing silhouette.

My effort here is to point out that stylizing is not a rigid thing, but a broad spectrum of possibilities. The only requirement is that the changes from realism be based on a style or form that attracts the eye. Simple distortion of a figure is *not* stylizing; there must be a discernible plan or reason, or the work itself will simply be crude.

Figs. 26–28 (clockwise from left). These three stylizations by T. E. Haag show a wide range of stylization. The figure of the girl at left merely omits details in face, feet and musculature, and possibly extends the legs to attain flow. The pedestal figure (below), on the other hand, suggests the curves of the human body and uses the hairline and buttocks as part of the design, but is otherwise barely recognizable. The third figure has a human face and shape that suggests a blocky male, but is otherwise composed largely of geometric designs.

Fig. 27.

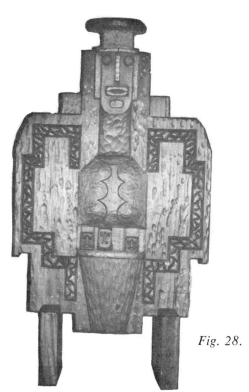

Fig. 28.

Fig. 29. Newlyweds, *by Mato Generalić, Yugoslavia, was carved in 1967. The flowers and the possessive hand of the groom are distorted and the faces are provided with insipid grins, making this a stylized caricature. It is about 3 ft (91 cm) tall.*

Fig. 30. Measuring, *by Milan Stanisavljević, is full of symbolism added to a distorted figure. The shoes are pans of a balance that also suggests the genitals, and the tongue is pierced by links on a fish scale and clamped to the head. Note particularly that one ear is a face and that the eyes are distorted to create the effect of timidity or sadness.*

Fig. 31. All the Same, *also by Milan Stanisavljević and carved in 1975, is symbolic stylizing, in which one hand and one foot are interchanged and an extra head is added between the legs.*

CHAPTER V
Some Nautical Mobiles

Model boats and burgees as Christmas-tree decorations

A PROFESSIONAL MAY BE ASKED TO CARVE some rather unusual things—which sometimes involve more painting, model-making or cabinetmaking than actual carving. These Christmas-tree decorations, for a family very much concerned with sailing, are a case in point. They are really individual mobiles, and offer ideas for other carvers who want to do something different.

Designs for the 22 yacht-club burgees, or identifying flags, were taken from a piece of fabric, but are also available in yachting books. They were sawed from ¼-in (6.4-mm) plywood, varnished, then painted with oils in the three American-flag colors of red, white and blue (or two of these three). To give them a little flair, each has a stub mast of gilded ¼-in (6.4-mm) dowel nailed to its inner edge.

Of the ship models, one, about 4 in (10 cm) long, was carved as a double-sided low-relief silhouette in mahogany; the others are assemblies with separately carved hulls, masts and spars of split bamboo from a discarded window shade. Sails are of exotic veneer woods carrying identifying symbols made with oil paints, while rudders and centerboards—or dagger boards—were whittled from birch tongue-depressors and inserted in whittled mahogany hulls. Tillers were whittled from toothpicks. Tallest of the boat models is about 7 in (18 cm). Most elaborate is the Mako 17-ft (5.2-m) outboard in figure 36, with a plastic windscreen, a music-wire rail, seats cut from dowels set on brads and a whittled outboard engine with a rotating aluminum prop. It is about 4 in (10 cm) long.

All burgees and the two cruisers (Figs. 34 and 36) have miniature screw eyes at balance points, while the sailing models are suspended from wire hangers through holes in the tops of the sails, as near balance point as possible, so that they will hang in sailing position. Sailboats were sprayed with matte varnish after assembly to protect them in the event of moisture or mishap.

Fig. 32 (above). Iceboat (with red-and-white Manhasset Yacht Club burgee) and Dyer Dink® 10, a sailing dinghy. The iceboat, tallest of the models, has aluminum runners and is sloop-rigged (has two sails). They are of sen wood.

Fig. 33 (right). Sunfish®, left, and Sol Cat® (catamaran or double-hulled boat). The Sunfish has a tigerwood sail, while the catamaran's are walnut.

Figs. 34–35 (above and right). Bertram 28-ft (8.5-m) cruiser is a low-relief double-sided silhouette in mahogany, about 4 in (10 cm) long, and the only model showing water. Water and glazing are lightened with white pigment, rubbed down.

28' Bertram Cruiser
Low-relief silhouette
Mahogany 3/8" thick

Fig. 36 (below). Mako 17 (left), Blue Jay (lerado sails), Laser International (jungle aspen sail) and Cape Dory 14 (commonly used for frostbite sailing in the winter, with striped sail—which is tinted veneer).

Figs. 37–40 (above and below, and on facing page). Burgees are uniform in size, 2¾ × 4 in (7 × 10 cm), with ¼-in (6.4-mm) gilded dowels for stub masts, but differ widely in coloration—as would be expected. They are more painted than carved. Colors are red, white and blue pigments mixed with gloss marine varnish, two coats for opacity. Identification names were lettered on the lower edges.

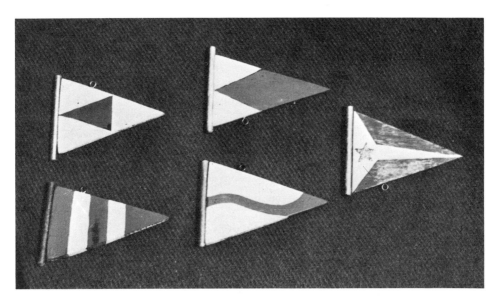

Fig. 39.

Fig. 40.

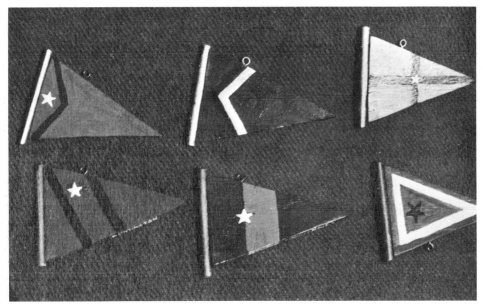

CHAPTER VI
"Bad" Wood Can Be Beautiful

Unusual sculpture from scraps and waste pieces

MOST CABINETMAKERS REJECT OR REPAIR any flawed or abnormal section of wood. Woodcarvers, however, can often capitalize on flaws such as knots and dry rot, or holes, lines and other deformities caused by insects or worms, to say nothing of unusual root or driftwood shapes. Some years ago, I carved animals in a low-relief spiral around a section of apple-tree trunk, exploiting natural projections, and got a much more dramatic effect than if I'd cut them away. I have since carved sections of trunks distorted by vines or other interferences, done a "bug tree" with designs around worm holes and rotted spots, and made cups and bowls of apple burls and sculptures of roots and cypress knees. I even have one client who intentionally selected boards with knots for panels! Two examples of these are the Nativity and the walnut polyglot of fruits and vegetables in Chapters 13 and 17.

Study a piece with an unusual shape or some intriguing defect; the result may be much more than salvage. I have selected several examples. One is a statuette from a vine-distorted branch, another a lion with mane created by insect infestation of a South American tree, and the third is a toad carved in dry-rotted, curly broadleaf maple, along with two cypress knees converted into statuettes (Figs. 44 and 45).

Pieces of bough like the lion's head are sold in Latin-American markets; they are found by Indians who sometimes carve them into Indian heads, with American Sioux headdresses from the distorted areas, and other designs, depending upon shape. In a sense, this is the same idea as that of American carvers of driftwood, diamond willow and rotted wood.

The toad in figure 43 was suggested by the shape of the piece I was given, and by the beauty of the wood itself. The top had a slope like a seated frog or toad, but the patterning of the wood definitely suggested a warty toad rather than a smooth frog; the greyed creamy color also supported this choice. While Americans collect frogs in many materials, and abhor toads, Orientals consider toads lucky. I have a toad carved in cryptomeria (Japanese "cedar" finished by sandblasting to make growth rings stand out), a netsuke in ivory from Japan—these were once used as thong buttons on pursestrings—and a red-stone toad from China, atop a stamp with my name in Chinese characters and the symbol with which I sign carvings.

This kind of wood is often so beautiful in itself that carving detracts rather than helps. I felt this was true of the maple block used for the toad carving, so most of the surface is uncarved and serves as a pillar or base. I finished the toad with satin varnish, and the base with gloss to stress its appearance. The varnish also reinforces the areas of the wood that tend to crumble at a touch. I originally carved bulging eyes from the wood, but replaced them with small grey-pearl-finished glass pendants for more gleam. Black-enamel spots were painted on for pupils, and then the pendants set-in so only oval shapes are visible. These pendants, incidentally, can be found at any notions store, and cost less by the dozen than would one set of glass eyes.

Dry-rotted wood, incidentally, is that which has been infected by decay fungi to an extent sufficient to cause discoloration, creating in the better pieces a marbled appearance on smooth surfaces. Because deterioration of the cell structure by the fungi is progressive, condition of the wood varies from apparently sound to noticeably softened and crumbly. If the wood is dried, the decay stops; but the fungi can remain dormant for years. Thus, if the wood again achieves a moisture content of 20 percent or so, the fungi may develop again and continue the process. This dry rot cannot occur except in the presence of moisture; thus, it is really *wet* rot.

Fig. 41. Lion head carved on a scrap of Chilean or Peruvian wood from a native market. Natives say such abnormal growth is caused by insects or fungus infection.

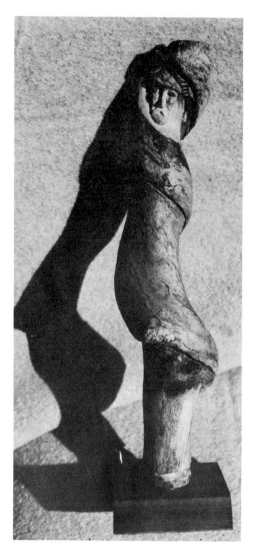

Fig. 42 (left). Windswept, carved in a section of branch distorted by a vine. It is about 15 in (38 cm) tall, with actual carving only around the face.

Fig. 43 (right). Toad atop a columnar base, all of spalted curly broadleaf maple. The toad is about 2 in (5.1 cm) high, on a spectacularly patterned 3¼ × 4 × 5-in (8.3 × 10 × 13-cm) base. Eyes are glass.

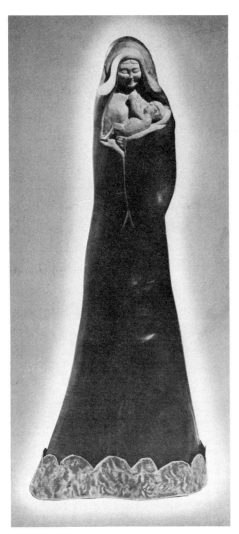

Fig. 44 (left). Madonna and Child carved in a cypress knee, about 15 in (38 cm) tall, with hammered-copper base strap. Again, the only carving is at the top. Knees have brown inner bark atop white growth wood, so contrast is marked.

Fig. 45 (right). Centaur and oread carved from a cypress knee. The figure is about 8 in (20 cm) tall.

CHAPTER VII
Ethnic or National Carving

It emphasizes the unusual (to us) in features, dress, site

SOMBRERO: MEXICAN. BERET: FRANCE. Wooden shoes: Netherlands. Feathers: Indian. Fez: Turkey. Flat hat: Spain. We are all quite familiar with such national or ethnic symbols. There are, of course, dozens more, but in any kind of art, they often bring to mind one particular race or ethnic group. Also, such appurtenances are used by ethnic or native artists to identify their own people as distinct from others. Costumes in general, weapons, activities and tools have changed, but certain identifying elements

Americans are given to carving cowboys, Indians, fishermen, pioneers, farmers and soldiers from past wars, each identified more by costume and pose than by face or figure. Other nations and ethnic groups do the same thing.

This group of figures explains what I mean. The first (Fig. 46) is one of my own, carved in Mexico from a piece of donated wood called *breal*. It is soft, fairly dense and very white, but with a thick red bark. The piece I was given suggested to me the flowing lines of a skirt, so I carved a statuette of one of the most colorful of Mexican types, a Tehuana—a woman of Tehuantepec, on the Isthmus. The town is ruled by its women, who are renowned for their beauty, statuesque carriage, height and unique costumes. Their costume includes a headdress made from the starched and pleated dress of a child; it is worn with the sleeves hanging down in back during the week, but on Sunday it is reversed so that the ruffled skirt forms an aureole and one sleeve hangs down the back, one in front. The wearer of this surprising headdress also wears a skirt billowed out by many petticoats.

The Ecuadorian male dancer in figure 48 is unique in a country that produces almost all carvings in quantity for sale to tourists. He is *not* a cowboy, but a dancer playing the part of a cowgirl in one of their almost endless Indian dance-pageants. The dance may go on for three days at a

Fig. 48 (below). Tipsy male dancer (note upturned eyeballs) has pushed his female mask aside for a restoring pull at the bottle. He is 12 in (30 cm) tall, from Ibarra, Ecuador, and carved in walnut. The texturing of his chaps—to suggest shaggy hide—is well done, and his costume, including a rope whip, is quite detailed.

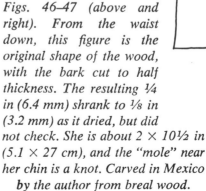

Figs. 46–47 (above and right). From the waist down, this figure is the original shape of the wood, with the bark cut to half thickness. The resulting ¼ in (6.4 mm) shrank to ⅛ in (3.2 mm) as it dried, but did not check. She is about 2 × 10½ in (5.1 × 27 cm), and the "mole" near her chin is a knot. Carved in Mexico by the author from breal wood.

time, with stops only for a bracing pull at the "puro" bottle. (This dancer is doubly prepared—he has a spare bottle in his hip pocket.) From a carving standpoint, there is the challenging problem here in contrasting the male and somewhat brutish face of a tipsy dancer with the sweet, innocent girlish face of the mask. Also, note the texturing of the chaps, made shaggy with random fluter cuts.

The Ona Indian strangling an ostrich (Fig. 49) has a similar technique on his hair and skirt, as well as on the long feathers of the bird. Cuts are varied here, however, through use of fluter, veiner, V-tool and larger gouges. His smooth skin is emphasized by texturing his costume. This figure, in mahogany stained even darker, was carved by Villalba, best of the present-day Argentine carvers. Note that the ostrich has been caught with a *boladero*, two weighted balls on opposite ends of a rope thrown to entangle the prey's feet.

The figa was originally an African fertility symbol, but has become the unofficial national symbol of Brazil. It is carved in wood or crystal, and cast in gold, silver or brass to be worn as a pendant. This combination of a figa with the head of a planter is an unusual depiction, but shows what the carver sees as a "typical" Brazilian. Other heads that display native opinion include a Hawaiian head about 3 in (7.6 cm) tall that I bought—of all places—in Alaska (Fig. 51), and the somewhat oversized head of a Balinese nude in figure 52, showing restrained Oriental characteristics. Also included are a Villalba head of an Argentine gaucho (Fig. 53), and the bearded figure of Holgar Danske in Copenhagen, legendary hero of the Danes (Fig. 54).

Not only people are carved with ethnic characteristics; the same is done with animals and scenes, sometimes using historical allusions of one kind or another. Among the examples shown are a pair of Indians in a canoe (Fig. 57) from Nicaragua, and, in figure 58, a Chilean cowboy's self-portrait, a Bolivian rendering of a llama and a Tierra del Fuego Ona Indian's self-portrait in calafate wood (from a bush producing berries which, if eaten, will make the visitor return, the natives say).

Fig. 49 (right). An Ona Indian of Patagonia strangles a ñandu (small ostrich) that he has bagged with his boladeros (weighted balls on the ends of a cord). Texturing of hair, skirt and feathers is random cutting with several gouges and a V-tool. The figure is caoba wood (mahogany) and is 11½ in (29 cm) tall with a 4½-in (11-cm) square base.

Fig. 50 (left). Figa, a fist with the thumb thrust between the second and third fingers, is a good luck symbol in Brazil. It is usually worn as a pendant, but this one is 10 in (25 cm) tall, thrust upward, and emerges from the hat of a typical farmer (who is usually European in origin). Textured hat brim and beard set off the smoothness of the arm and hand. Fingernails are shown, but the hand has no creases.

Figs. 51–52 (left and below). Hawaiian male and Balinese female, as their own people see them. Note the differences in hair treatment and eyes, but similarity in noses and foreheads. The male statuette was bought in Alaska, the female in Bali.

Fig. 53 (right). Villalba, premier Argentine wood-carver, produced both of these figures, which are basically tourist items. Both are a lighter wood, painted black. Note, however, the strength of the bust head, with long moustache, short beard and a headband over chopped-off hair.

Fig. 54 (left). Holgar Danske is a legendary Danish hero. Here he is shown as a brooding figure with long hair and unkempt beard, head down rather than defiant.

Figs. 55–56 (above and left). Confederate soldier by Howard Green, Houston, Texas, is a one-piece carving of yellow pine. It is a dynamic pose, with essential detail and no hint of caricature.

Fig. 57 (above). A Nicaraguan Indian carved this pirogue with husband and wife. Note wide skulls and the simple but powerful body structure. Fig. 58 (below). Three figures from South America illustrate self images. At left is a Chilean cowboy, and at right is an Ona Indian, of extreme southern Argentina. The center carving is a Bolivian's treatment of a llama, beast-of-all-burdens down there.

CHAPTER VIII
Likenesses of Professions

Very visible craft figures are well displayed on a maypole

THE MAIBAUM OR MAYPOLE IS A FAMILIAR DECORATION in Bavarian towns, and is often very decorative. It dates back to pagan times and was used in May Day dances in which the dancers interwove long ribbon streamers pendant from the pole top. The German poles may have a ring on a top swivel from which the streamers are hung, but they also have a series of arms up the sides of the pole bearing silhouette figures.

Silhouettes of the occupations of typical villagers and the city seal are common forms. Georg Keilhofer produced such a pole for the city of Frankenmuth, Michigan, several years ago. It has two hand-carved crests, one for the city and one for Gunzenhausen, its sister city in Bavaria; the other ten carvings depict the various occupations. All are silhouette relief carvings, painted in bright colors and set on arms extending from the central pole, which is like a utility pole painted with a blue-and-white spiral.

Figures for uses such as this must be designed with a dramatic silhouette, so they will stand out against any background. It is also advisable to make them of thick wood, both for durability and to permit deep relief carving on both sides so shadow effects are obtained to supplement the color. Figures like these must be kept simple and yet be fairly formal, because members of the professions involved will not take kindly to public kidding, or even ridicule, which much caricature tends to be.

(opposite page)

Figs. 59–60 (left to right). The Maibaum, by Georg Keilhofer. From the top, left to right, are: Baker, Miller, Spinning Lady, Carpenter, Chef, Butcher, Bricklayer, Blacksmith, Lumberman, Farmer, and crests for the cities of Frankenmuth and Gunzenhausen. (Photo courtesy of Frankenmuth Bavarian Inn, Inc.)

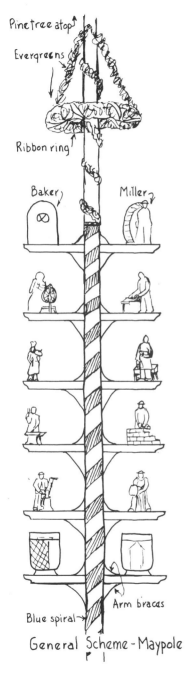

Pinetree atop

Evergreens

Ribbon ring

Baker   Miller

Blue spiral

Arm braces

General Scheme - Maypole

CHAPTER IX

Three "Different" Birds

Nonrealism serves a purpose—for emphasis or humor

HAVING MADE MY QUOTA OF RELATIVELY SIMPLE painted birds some years ago, I have had more admiration for than interest in birds in recent years. However, I have on occasion made bird caricatures, panels of low-relief bird carvings and the like. Three recent and rather unusual examples are shown here.

The first is a stooping eagle or hawk. It is somewhat stylized in that the wings are accentuated and the body shortened for effect. Also, only the general shape and outline of the wings are carved; the feathering is left to the imagination of the observer. While I have indicated how the feathering might be stylized in the sketch, I do not consider it a necessity. It may actually be confusing to the observer since a bird alighting is shape and color, and not detailed feathering—your eyes can't see individual feathers, even from a few feet away. The bird is in pine and finished with a Beiz (salammoniac) German stain.

The other two birds (Figs. 63 and 64) are, nominally, stylized owls. The idea was born when I received an owl blank in paulownia wood—from a decorative tree introduced into this country some years ago and now coming into commercial use as well—which is similar to butternut in color and texture. I carved a stylized owl on one side of the blank and then varied it by carving a cat head on a bird body on the other, thus producing a "catbird" of sorts. I went on to make another blank (this time of pine) and carved it similarly, except that the head on the reverse of the second one was that of a bull, producing a bullfinch, cowbird or "cowl," as you wish. In these two instances, the horns of the cow and the ears of the cat match the feather tufts of the owl, and create no problems. There may be other birds that can be similarly caricatured, but I haven't thought of them.

It is possible to make other caricatures to match catfish, dogfish, devilfish and cowfish by carving an appropriate head in the round on a fish body rather than making the carving double-sided. Such a group could be combined in an amusing mobile. Finishing can be simple stain or colors.

A related idea is a recognizable silhouette of a fish or a frog of, say, ¾-in (19-cm) pine, sawed into a jigsaw puzzle of blocky and interlocking letters. This may also be done with some names, if the name suggests a bird, flower, craft or anything that can be silhouetted.

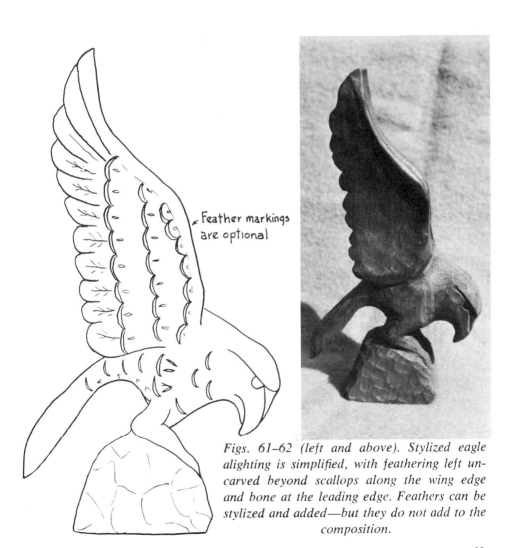

Feather markings are optional

Figs. 61–62 (left and above). Stylized eagle alighting is simplified, with feathering left uncarved beyond scallops along the wing edge and bone at the leading edge. Feathers can be stylized and added—but they do not add to the composition.

Figs. 63–64 (above and below). Two stylized owls in 2-in (5.1-cm) paulownia, at left, and Oregon pine at right, become a catbird and a cowbird when turned around.

CHAPTER X
Remember the Circus?

Acrobats, contortionists and balanced figures

LIKE MOST KIDS, I WAS INTERESTED IN acrobats and contortionists, and the interest stayed with me. Many years ago, I carved what is called an "ironjaw" in the circus—an acrobat who hangs from a wire by biting a pad in her mouth. I have used it as a light-cord pull ever since. Recently, I gave further vent to my interest in acrobats by whittling four figures, all in soft-wood scraps on an experimental basis. The first was a figure that would stand either on its hands or its feet, the second and third contortionists—with body formed into a loop, and with legs behind head—and the fourth an acrobat able to stand on either leg or either arm.

The two acrobat figures (Fig. 65) are primarily problems in balance; you must anticipate where the center of gravity of the finished carving will be and compensate for it, either in pose or by weighting the finished figure. The handstand is relatively simple, in that the projection of the buttocks in back can be compensated for by projecting the knees forward. Also, minor unbalance can be compensated for by tilting the entire figure slightly, so the hands should be left thick and carved only after the angle of the palms has been determined—so the figure stands securely erect. Remember that a balanced figure is really a lever, and that the effect of a lever is a combination of the lever-arm length and the weight at the end. Thus the projecting buttocks in back are balanced by a lesser weight projecting in the opposite direction at the knees because the lever arm is longer.

The four-way standing acrobat (Fig. 65) is much more complex to balance, because his extended leg is inevitably heavier than his frontally extended arm, and upper torso is inevitably heavier than lower limbs, particularly when one leg is out of place. Some compensation can be made by extending the hand in front and the leg in back to provide support *above* center—a hard pose for the foot because it extends downward of itself (which is the wrong direction for balance). Also, the body viewed from the front will be heavier on one side than the other because of the torso and upward- and downward-extended limbs. You must compensate for this as well by centering the hand or foot under the body rather than extending it straight out. Try standing on one foot, and you'll see what I mean; the body automatically shifts to center itself over the supporting foot—or you fall down. Thus, each arm and leg must be carved so that the hand or foot is at least at the body centerline. I suggest that you leave the hands and feet oversize and carve them last, compensating for unbalance. Tilting the supporting surface of a hand or foot sideways as well as forward or back will help in this, and the final shaping can be done to match.

I found it necessary to supplement all this by adding scrap-silver bracelets on one arm and anklets on one ankle for more stability. (Silver is 20 times as heavy as the same volume of wood, iron only 15.) In any case, the balancing is a tricky and lengthy process you must consider from the original design right through to final carving.

Of the two contortionists in figure 66, the one tied in a knot is in proper proportion, and the body in a circle is somewhat stylized to obtain the ring. Human legs actually will bend at the knee and ankle, not in between. On the circular figure, the head must be drawn back slightly, or the nose may be damaged by bumping. My idea is to combine these two figures in a mobile some day.

From a whittling standpoint, it doesn't matter much which way grain runs on the contortionists; it will cause some trouble on the circular figure regardless of direction, and on the knotted figure, vertical grain is helpful when carving the feet. On the acrobats, grain runs with the body.

You can go ahead and detail muscles, rib cages and the like—they certainly are visible in figures strained as these are. And you can add clothing as you like where possible, preferably by painting on leotards, shorts or whatever. Sex of the figures can suit your fancy.

Fig. 65 (above). Acrobats are carved to balance however they stand, the one at right on hands or feet, the one at left in any of four positions. Note silver band on ankle and wrist to add stability. Fig. 66 (below). Contortionists form a ring and a ball; the figure at right has his feet locked behind his head. Both are in pine.

Fig. 67 (right). An "ironjaw" hangs by her mouth in the circus, but makes a light-pull for me. She is also pine, but was carved some years ago and has darkened from handling.

CHAPTER XI
Masks Can Be Very Different

Three examples offer startling possibilities

MASKS OFFER A PARTICULARLY INTERESTING FIELD for doing the unusual, in materials, shapes, coloring and finishing. The masks pictured here are no exception, though they certainly are exceptional—in more ways than one!

The first is a reversible mask, which can be worn in either of two differing expressions. I made it from an old basswood pattern that a friend donated, hollowing out the back first so that the eyes could be located to fit my own. (In many masks, the wearer looks through slits below or above the eyes carved in the mask, enabling the carver to incorporate unusual eyes in his design.) The old childhood stunt of making a head that rotates to depict a smile or a frown was given a new dimension here by the natural shape of the blank, which enabled me to carve one head with a beard—which becomes hair on the other—and one somewhat feminine. I finished the head with flat stain, but you may want to paint it in colors. Interestingly enough, when we look at a face, we tend to look first at the eyes and then look *below* them, not above. Thus, it matters little that there is a peculiar shape to this mask's forehead.

My two other examples are elongated caricatures carved from red oak and hollowed—not to be worn, but as a standing or hanging decoration to be lighted inside. It makes a very dramatic decoration in a room, and is guaranteed to start a conversation. Though most normal masks can be hung and lighted similarly, a visibly hewn caricature is somehow more effective.

Masks may incorporate many other materials. Mexican masks often incorporate horse or dog teeth, animal skins for hair or beard, colored glass marbles for eyes, and so on. The Balinese carve caricatured ears, teeth, noses and such and combine them with ribbons, paper or both used for tongues. Other masks may depict two faces at once—of twins, or of differing moods or sexes—as in some African ceremonial ones. They may include elaborate headdresses or hairdos.

Fig. 68 (left). Life-size mask in stained pine is reversible—either a male head with beard or a fat-cheeked female.

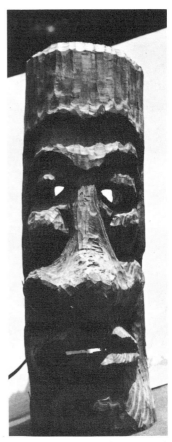

Figs. 69–70 (above and left). Caricature in oak half-log, 5½ × 22 in (14 × 56 cm), is not intended for wearing, but is hollowed for interior lighting as a standing or wall decoration. Tool lines are left to give it a "chopped-out" appearance.

CHAPTER XII
Children Can Be Angels

They are, when Ruth Hawkins carves them

RUTH HAWKINS IS A VERY MODEST, UNASSUMING mountain carver who sells her work through the Campbell Folk School at Brasstown, North Carolina. Many other carvers do the same thing, but most of them follow patterns provided by the school; she follows her own, which are unique both in design and technique. All of her designs are children or child angels. All are whittled (she uses only a knife) from holly ⅛ to 3/16 in (3.2 to 4.7 mm) thick. And all are low-relief, meticulously detailed in contrast to the usual Campbell in-the-round figures. They are in theory Christmas-tree silhouette ornaments, but are usually snapped up by collectors for year-round display.

Her work has been widely copied by others—including me—but the copies, as usual, lose just a little of the piquancy and dash of the original. Ruth is not concerned about copies; as one admirer asserts, "If she knew you were copying one of her figures, she'd probably offer to help."

I have attempted to sketch about half of her designs, and have pictured some that I copied as well as two of her originals. When I finish this, I'm going to try again (I just haven't quite gotten the faces right, to say nothing of the hair and hands). And I hope some day to get my hands on one design that is totally unique—a satanic little imp in mahogany or some other dark wood, which I suspect Ruth carved once when her own kids were belying her images of them!

Fig. 71.

Fig. 72 (above). Eight copies of Ruth Hawkins' figures by the author, whittled from ⅛-in (3.2-mm) holly and finished by waxing. Surfaces are thinned and contoured behind faces, hands and so on to avoid a "thick" look. Fig. 73 (below). Ruth Hawkins carved the light and winsome figures at upper right and lower left; I carved the comparatively crude copy at upper left, a student the one at lower right.

CHAPTER XIII
Unusual Nativity Scenes

Silhouettes, stylized and "sliver" figures—all whittled

NATIVITY SCENES CAN INCLUDE SHEPHERDS, sheep, cows, cowherds, Mary's donkey, the Magi, camels, cherubim, angels, doves, the Star of Bethlehem and even the Little Drummer Boy. I have carved several, of varying size. Goethe talked of the extravagant ones he saw in Florence; I've seen one in Mexico with more than a hundred figures, including both the Last Supper and Christ on the cross—a bit ahead of itself, to say the least! In this case, however, I assayed two different approaches (Figs. 74–81): one with highly stylized figures, the other with flat silhouettes spaced out on a base to give the effect of a scene with depth.

Those in the stylized group (Figs. 74–77) have standardized faces, basically a double arc for the eyebrows enclosing a tapered block for the nose between them. I made my samples from scraps of pine, basswood and jelutong, and found that this mixture gave so much variety in color and texture that I had to tint all the figures with light-colored stains—two red, two brown. Individual figures are easy to whittle because they avoid the usual problem with hands and faces.

The other set was carved in holly ⅛ to ³⁄₁₆ in (3.2 to 4.7 mm) thick, each figure a low-relief silhouette. I eventually carved the Magi on both sides and mounted them individually like chessmen, so they could be placed with more freedom. The Holy Family and the donkey were glued to the base or stage, a 1 × 3 × 9-in (2.54 × 7.6 × 23-cm) walnut block, fronting a background of walnut ¾ × 9 × 9 in (1.9 × 23 × 23 cm). The background, incidentally, was scrapped by a local cabinetmaker because it included a central, prominent knot. This, however, made an attractive suggestion of a mountain or hill, and provided a mounting surface for the star, two flying doves and an angelic choir.

All figures in this scene are relatively small. Joseph is only 3 in (7.6 cm) tall, and the tallest Magus is 3½ in (8.9 cm) atop a ½-in (13-mm) base.

Shepherds and sheep are mounted on a ⅜ × 2¾ × 8-in (.9 × 7 × 20-cm) walnut scrap as a group; it gives them relative position and keeps them from falling over. They were positioned by putting their baseboard in front of the stage on which the Holy Family had been glued, and setting them so that they face the manger without obstructing the frontal view of the Holy Family. Note that individual figures do not have to be parallel with the background. They can be angled to suit the scene, as long as the angle is not so great that it reveals how thin they are. The shepherd group thus gives the effect of in-the-round figures, which can be removed and replaced by the Magi for Epiphany or used with them. They also make an interesting and less-deep variation from the standard scene, which often can't be placed on the available shelf.

Holly figures were finished with a sealant and neutral Kiwi® shoe polish, which gives a desirable low gloss and protects the almost dead-white wood from soiling. Holly, incidentally, is sufficiently close-grained to support as much detail as you wish. English sycamore is a good alternative, and other woods, such as maple, can be used if the size of the figures is increased. This group was sold before it was finished.

Fig. 74. Stylized figures of Joseph, 4 in (10 cm) tall, two shepherds and the Babe in the manger. All have simplified faces and no hand details.

Fig. 75 (above). Two sheep and two shepherds—one with lamb, the other with a crook. Again, there is tinting but no detailing.

Fig. 76 (below). The Three Wise Men, or Magi, include one standing figure and two kneeling in different ways.

Fig. 77 (above). The combined stylized group includes ten figures. Fig. 78 (below). Basic low-relief Nativity figures are Joseph, Mary, the manger, and possibly the donkey. These are of holly, ⅛ in (3.2 mm) thick, with Joseph only 3 in (7.6 cm) tall.

Fig. 79 (above). Shepherds, also of ⅛-in (3.2-mm) holly, can vary widely in number and pose. Here we have three, one with crook and one with lamb, plus four sheep. Note that figures are mounted at angles, which helps to compose the overall scene. Their platform, lower than that of the Holy Family, keeps them upright. Fig. 80 (below). The Magi, or Three Wise Men, are mounted separately and carved on both sides. Thus, they can be positioned as desired, and can either replace the shepherds after Epiphany or be part of the total group.

Fig. 81. The Holy Family, with shepherd group, mounted on a stage with sloping edges and against a 9 × 9-in (23 × 23-cm) background that carries doves, the Star of Bethlehem and a three-angel choir. Base for the Holy Family is higher than that for shepherds and Magi, and their background includes a central knot.

In recent years, both Swiss and German carvers have stylized religious subjects, partly to get away from the very elaborate detailing of the conventional Baroque figures, and partly to speed carving. It substitutes line and shadow for tinting and avoids some of the fragile detail of older designs. To illustrate the basic concept, I have pictured here two modern stylized figures from the designs of Hans Hüggler-Wyss, of Brienz, Switzerland (Fig. 82), as well as two of the miniature scenes formerly made with "sliver" figures in Oberammergau, Germany (Fig. 83). These figures were once tourist items sold for very low prices, but are no longer available because labor costs and exchange rates have both raised the price beyond an economical amount. The sliver figures are actually very highly stylized, and are produced from pine scraps with a few carefully oriented slashes per figure.

Fig. 82 (above). Two of the modern simplified and stylized low-gloss figures, about 6 in (15 cm) tall, carved from pine and tinted in Brienz, Switzerland. Angles and lines replace detail—Christ, at left, has only the general outlines of face and hands. Fig. 83 (below). Two groups of "sliver figures" from Oberammergau, W. Germany. The one at right includes only Mary, Joseph, the Babe and the Star in half a walnut shell, and the Crucifixion in the other half. That at left shows shepherds and Magi in fold-out doors of a turned-walnut case, with Joseph, Mary, the manger and angels in the central portion. All have stars overhead. Once upon a time, the shell group sold for a dollar and the group at left for less than five.

Figs. 84–85 (above and left). For comparison, here are two of the Three Wise Men for an elaborate traditional Nativity scene being carved by Howard Green, Houston, Texas. They are larger, and in a better wood and thus are not tinted or painted.

CHAPTER XIV
A Scene to Order

Relief combined with stylized wilderness for an effect

WOODCARVINGS OF SPECIFIC SCENES and people can be challenging to any carver, because they usually involve foliage, may include water and clouds, and can be expected to achieve at least approximate likenesses. The usual in-the-round treatment of such a subject tends to be a caricature, and a very stiff one at that. A relief panel offers better prospects, but can be difficult as well. Thus, it is advisable to make a series of compromises, possibly arriving at an unusual solution or depiction.

Fig. 86. Mahogany panel, ¾ × 12 × 19 in (1.9 × 30 × 48 cm), is made from a century-old table leaf, so patina is preserved in framing and brush on the shore at top.

This panel will serve as an example. It was a commission, a birthday present for the lady of the carving from her husband. It was to depict them in their canoe, not on Long Island Sound where they commonly paddle, but at an island in northern Maine. No pictures were available of the island, the canoe or its occupants, but the canoe is a standard Grumman® 17 and the occupants are friends, so there was a starting point.

There are several books on canoeing with pictures of two people in a canoe, as well as pictures of this particular canoe, so a rough sketch could be made. Once this was finished, the client made several criticisms: I had seated him too far forward; I had changed the point of view from that in the pictures, raising it slightly so more of the legs of both people were visible; I'd made the paddles too short; instead of the flat shoreline I'd drawn, there should've been a curved one, with a bluff and rocks, and over the bluff a tangle in which birch, an apple and an oak could be distinguished at designated points; there were no pines, and, at the left, there should've been an edge with an overhang. There should also have been a slight bow wave and a small wake as well, he suggested.

These alterations were put on the sketch, which was then adapted to a piece of old mahogany ¾ × 12 × 19 in (1.9 × 30 × 48 cm). I arbitrarily decided to lower the ground ½ in (13 mm) around the canoe, leaving wood for the bow wave and wake, as well as for the eddy where the visible paddle enters the water. Only the lower portion was grounded, initially.

Water can be difficult to depict—if you try to be too specific. It is much easier to *suggest* wavelets by leaving the background rough and texturing it with a small-diameter flat gouge, say a ½-in (13-mm) No. 4 or 5. The curvature of the canoe was shaped to clear the visible paddle, show the precise position of bow wave and wake, and to get a proper meeting line between canoe and water. Bad meeting lines, between such objects as a house and the ground in front of it, are a common error in low-relief panels. Here, the curvature of the canoe itself makes the solution obvious. The canoe surface is brought down to the water; there is no step between.

When rough shaping of figures and canoe were completed, it was possible to go back and do the shoreline, indenting it irregularly and establishing the rocks along the shore to match the client's description. Again, the rocks had to be sloped on their lower surfaces so that they met the water without too much step, and cut back near the male figure to help him stand out. Some visible shoreline (where the sand itself meets the water) was also included to establish perspective. To get the effect of an overhang and erosion, the "vertical" portion of the bank was sharply indented along the top. This idea was enhanced by showing a side view of the overhang at the left-hand upper end. This takes some juggling, and requires that you stand back and look at the entire panel frequently as you work.

Because the panel was old mahogany—it had been the center of a small table for over a hundred years—the surface had a dark and attractive patina, which had to be sacrificed for the water area and the principal subject. By trenching in at the edges, I could leave a darker border or frame on three sides, along with a V-tooled, border-defining line I had carved along the top.

It seemed rather absurd to attempt carving a Maine wilderness atop the island when the center of interest should be the canoe. So the bush area was simply stylized with irregular lines, although portions of the boles of the three special trees were made visible in suitable locations and identified by branching and bark texture. The birch, for example, could be carved so that the dark patches indicating one-time small branches could be left while the patina is cut away to lighten the rest. On the oak, there are vertical lines simulating bark markings and high-up branching. On the apple, there is a shorter trunk and a visible crotch. This worked out quite well, and saved a great deal of time, energy and likely disappointment.

The finished piece was given a spray coat of satin varnish as a sealant, followed by two coats of Kiwi® neutral shoe polish. (Conventional waxes tend to load open-grain woods like mahogany and eventually create grey speckles, unless the entire surface is filled.)

CHAPTER XV
Carving a Scene to Fit

Miniature figures are provided with a background

A QUARTER OF A CENTURY AGO, my younger sister sent me a set of whittled figures from Bavaria. Each was about ¾ in (19 mm) tall, in national costume, and doing something identifiable. I vowed to make a background for them, a panel in which they could be mounted. Some years back, I made stools, chairs and tables for them, in scale. I have—at long last—produced the background as well.

It is carved 1 in (2.54 cm) or so deep in a 2 × 7 × 19-in (5.1 × 18 × 48-cm) length of Oregon pine, and is really a composite of three photographs and some fill-in scenery like pine trees to provide an area for the four woodsmen in the group. One background unit is a Gasthaus or inn in the Virgen valley, East Tyrol, along with a Salzburg farmstead and a Swiss village in Valais. All were selected and combined because they are approximately the right angle and scale for assembly, which was more important to me than having all three pictures from the same small area of the Alps.

Fig. 87. A 2 × 7 × 19-in (5.1 × 18 × 48-cm) pine panel carved 1 in (2.54 cm) deep and painted, provides both a scenic background and perspective for the figures. Nine are near the inn at right, three in front of the chalet at left, the cheese seller is climbing the path to the village and four woodsmen are in the forest.

Fig. 88 (left). These whittled and painted figures, each about ¾ in (19 mm) tall, were brought from Bavaria a quarter-century ago. They include eight beer drinkers, four woodsmen, three people with whips, a waiter and a cheese peddler. Stools, benches and chairs were made to scale some years ago.

Standing figures came mounted on small clear-plastic bases, and had either to be removed from the bases or posed on a level area. I chose the latter because the figures would be unnaturally tilted if mounted on a slope. I also found that, as carving progressed, I had to modify my original plan to maintain perspective. First, the picture showed a sloping court in front of the inn (camera-lens distortion). I had to have it flat to take two tables and

Fig. 89. A closeup of the area near the chalet, showing four of the figures.

70

Fig. 90 (above). Three separate photos, inn at right, chalet and village at left, were combined with a general Alpine background and pine forest to make the scene and provide locations for all of the figures. Here the inn has been carved, the chalet begun and the background village sketched in on a lowered ground. Fig. 91 (below). Further carving brings out the forest and village, suggests that more of the chalet be exposed behind the hill to provide a platform for the people with whips.

eight or nine people. I needed another flat spot for the group of whippers, and decided to put that in front of the house so that people were somewhat distributed across the face of the panel. And the village—sketched on an eminence at upper left—was to smaller scale, so people were too big to go back there. (Figures in scale for the village would have had to be half or less the size of those in the foreground.) Finally, my original dense pine woods with paths leading to them had to be cut back to create two level areas for woodsmen, and a dip had to be added to the trail leading to the village so that the cheese peddler could be set fairly level.

This general scene has been carved for many years in various parts of the world. I have had examples from Germany, Mexico, Panama and Switzerland. Some are with people, some without. A kitchen scene is common because of the color possible in pots and pans, and usually the floor is tilted up to provide perspective, as it is in a photograph. In any case, however, a scene like this should probably be covered with glass; too many observers reach out to touch "the cute little people," dislodging or breaking them.

Painting is fairly straightforward. I used oils, but others can be substituted, as long as you remember that the colors should not be so brilliant that they overawe the figures. What's more, in an outdoor scene the colors are muted and greyed by distance. Thus, the trees and mountains in the background are not as brightly colored as the buildings and trees in the foreground.

CHAPTER XVI
Flowers, Birds and Insects

118 units in one low-relief panel

POLYGLOT PANELS CAN BE ADAPTED TO THE WOOD, both in shape and in content. The mahogany panel, for example, is carved in the left-over end from the central panel of an ancient table, well over a hundred years old when scrapped. Thus, the panel retains the curve and shaping of the table edge, even the long bevel that originally met the edge's arc, and there is a channel on the back. The original finish of the wood is retained in the borders as well. Carving is relatively shallow because the background is lowered less than ¼ in (6.4 mm).

The request, in this instance, was for a panel that would combine birds and flowers. I made scale somewhat smaller than in previous panels, so content is much greater—118 units, of which six are birds and 109 flowers, plus a gnome, a moth and a butterfly. As usual, I laid out the elements as I went, using flower and bird guides as sources. I tried to select familiar examples as far as possible, while still attaining a variety of shapes and textures adjacent to each other. The whole becomes somewhat of a jigsaw puzzle, and the danger is that units will be crowded too closely together, or that scale will be so small that detail cannot be attained. This is a particular problem with mahogany because of its tendency to split (even when it is the best grade of Honduras mahogany and as old as this is).

When laying out a panel of this sort, it is essential that an identifying key be retained. I make a list with names and reference page numbers on an adjacent piece of paper. I also lay out the designs themselves directly on the wood, and carve them about one line behind the layout before my original sketch becomes confusing or the references difficult to find. A key drawing can be made afterward, either with transparent paper over the carving itself or over an enlarged photograph, as I did in this instance. There is little need to make an accurate sketch, since the possibility of an exactly similar carving is remote.

Key to Mahogany Panel

1. Wild or blue lupine
2. Ruby-throated hummingbird
3. Showy lady's slipper
4. Common or great mullein
5. Ragged robin
6. Larger blue flag, blue iris, fleur-de-lis
7. African tulip
8. Tree hibiscus (tropical)
9. Jacaranda (tropical)
10. Turk's cap (tropical bush)
11. Red-tailed hawk
12. Violet wood sorrel
13. Moss or ground pink
14. Arethusa or Indian pink
15. Fringed polygala
16. Hibiscus (tropical tree)
17. Angel's trumpet (tropical tree)
18. Gnome riding the above
19. Chenille plant (tropical)
20. Queen Anne's lace, bird nest, wild carrot
21. Pitcher plant or huntsman's cup
22. Common mallow, or cheeseflower
23. Jewelweed, spotted touch-me-not
24. Wintergreen
25. Wild morning glory, hedge bindweed
26. Wild geranium or cranesbill
27. Lily of the valley
28. Wild ginger
29. Barn swallow
30. Red clover
31. White clover
32. Downy yellow violet
33. Pasture or swamp rose
34. Shooting star, American cowslip
35. Amaryllis (tropical)
36. Moneywort or myrtle
37. Broad-leaved arrow-head (watery)
38. Mud plantain (water plant)
39. White violet
40. Dogwood (a tree)
41. Pink azalea
42. Pickerel weed (watery)
43. Rose
44. Water parsnip
45. Luna moth
46. Evening primrose
47. Day lily
48. Field or Canada lily
49. Common milkweed
50. Blue violet
51. Purslane
52. Indian pipe (marshy)
53. Bird of paradise (tropical)
54. Bunchberry or dwarf cornel
55. Prickly pear (a cactus)
56. Goldenrod
57. Flicker
58. Ginger
59. Skullcap
60. Purple trillium
61. Torch lily or torch ginger (tropical)
62. Coral or trumpet honeysuckle
63. Swallowtail butterfly
64. Common sunflower
65. Blue jay
66. Purple virgin's bower
67. Cardinal flower
68. Indian tobacco
69. Blue-eyed grass
70. Pasque flower
71. Wild columbine
72. Jerusalem artichoke
73. Dandelion
74. Turtlehead
75. Thunbergia (tropical)
76. Blue toadflax
77. Blazing star
78. Chicory or succory
79. Bush honeysuckle
80. Atamasco lily
81. Anthurium (tropical)
82. Alocasia (tropical)
83. Purple coneflower
84. Bluet
85. Virgin's bower
86. Partridgeberry
87. Saw-whet owl
88. Robin's plantain
89. Star of Bethlehem
90. Monkshood or aconite
91. Bellflower
92. Pearly everlasting
93. Bull thistle
94. Purple thorn apple
95. Goldthread
96. Wood anemone
97. Indian pink, pinkroot
98. Cow lily or cowslip (water)
99. Water lily, water nymph
100. Large marsh pink, sabbatica
101. Harebell
102. Mountain laurel
103. American rhododendron
104. House wren
105. Sneezewort
106. Spring beauty
107. Water arum
108. Day flower
109. Jack-in-the-pulpit, Indian turnip
110. Spiderwort, Job's tears
111. Golden club
112. Skunk cabbage (marsh)
113. Common cattail (marsh)
114. Pink lady's slipper, moccasin flower
115. Bellwort
116. Fringed gentian
117. Burdock
118. Sea pink

Total: 1 gnome, 1 butterfly, 1 moth, 6 birds, 109 flowers

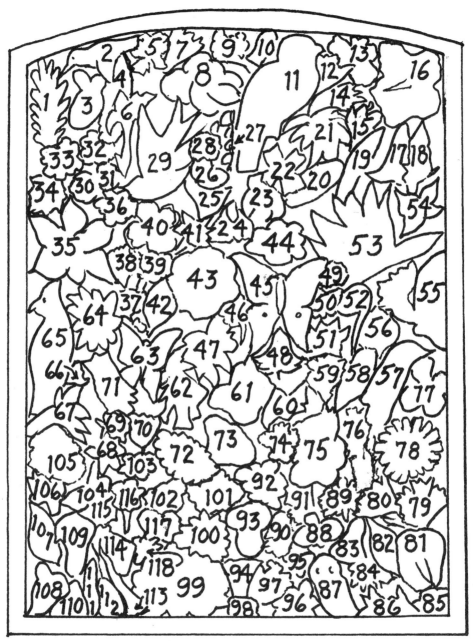

Fig. 92. Key to mahogany polyglot panel, which is ¾ × 11¾ × 16 in (1.9 × 30 × 41 cm) and retains edge curvature and shaping.

Fig. 93. The finished panel. Units are fitted together to minimize background and filler designs such as stems and branches. Background is stained darker.

CHAPTER XVII

Carve a Polyglot Panel

Familiar fruits and vegetables—step-by-step

AN OVERALL PANEL NORMALLY INVOLVES elaborate tracery of foliage or a grouping to tie the elements together. A polyglot panel, however, requires nothing but step-by-step carving of single subjects; the only problems are with making the elements approach or overlay each other. It does not require lengthy planning, sketching and designing, because the design develops as you carve. (I design or draw only one set of subjects ahead of my carving.) You can trace or otherwise copy all the elements without change of scale, providing there are enough potential subjects in the theme you select. And your selection of subjects and theme will also determine the level of difficulty you encounter. Further, this kind of carving provides a great deal of training in grounding out, shaping forms, and in texturing. The results are often unique.

In my first polyglot, the "bug tree," I was immediately faced with legs and antennae in profusion. Fortunately, scale was large. This fruit and vegetable panel is an easier way to start. The individual designs are familiar to all of us, with many distinctive shapes. You can avoid difficult forms or texturing, such as lettuce heads and parsley, if you prefer, and pictures or the objects themselves are readily available. There are at least again as many fruits and vegetables as the 63 I used—such familiar ones as lemon, orange, honeydew melon, parsnip and celery are not included.

Here, the client selected panel wood and shape. She liked the growth-wood color contrast and the sloping bevelled edge that resulted from the natural shape of the tree. Wood is black walnut, $1 \times 7\frac{3}{4} \times 16\frac{5}{8}$ in ($2.54 \times 20 \times 42$ cm) which is not particularly inclined to split, able to support considerable detail, and finishes well.

My source for almost all of the 63 designs was a handbook of fruits and vegetables from the local library. I altered scale in some cases because a watermelon and peppers create rather sharp size contrasts, and I used sliced sections in others because the whole fruit or vegetable would repeat a shape and be monotonous. A peach, a plum, and an apricot are basically alike except for color—and color is not available in a panel like this unless you use a light wood and tint it. Also, the interior of some fruits is much more interesting than the exterior from a design standpoint.

It is unnecessary to lower the background more than about ⅛ in (3.2 mm) in a small panel of this type. You don't have to undercut, either. There can be a border or frame if you wish, the entire panel can be trenched, or the edges cut away. I trenched at the sides because of the squared edges, and cut the border away at the top. Initially, I had planned to leave pristine the irregular top edge created by the natural curvature of the tree, but I ultimately put condiments there—parsley, pepper, dill and cinnamon—and carved them in intaglio to leave the dark grooved surface and add to the contrast with the rest of the panel. One virtue of this sort of design is that you can make such alterations as they occur to you. It is not even necessary to balance the two sides of the panel unless you wish to do so. I created a rough balance by putting the head lettuce on one side and the cauliflower on the other, and balancing the long diagonal line of the sugar beet at one top corner with that of the asparagus at the other. The fairly large and complex bunch of grapes was placed near the center to dominate the composition.

All through the panel, I overlapped drawings of subjects, and then decided which was to appear above the other when I was carving. In most instances, this decision is surprisingly easy because one subject has the overlap portion near the surface, while the other will curve away. The principal problem is to keep the background areas small and irregularly shaped, and to select subjects of contrasting shape and texture to go side by side. With a whole guide to pick from, that task is easy.

Tools required can be few and simple. I used a hook or pull knife, a V-tool, two veiners (one very small), ⅛-in (3.2-mm) firmer, ⅛- and ¼-in (3.2- and 6.4-mm) flat gouges, and a ¼-in (6.4-mm) half-round gouge. Larger half-round or semi-half-round gouges could be used to form rounded shapes like those of currants, grapes and cranberries, but I shaped them with a hook knife and left them slightly irregular. (A pro would use the gouge of proper size and shape to speed the work.) Practically all of the setting-in was done with the ⅛-in (3.2-mm) firmer, and grounding with the same tool in two steps: one roughing, one finishing. A light mallet controlled depth of setting-in and roughing, while smoothing the ground was done by hand. When setting-in, allow at least ¼ in (6.4 mm) of solid wood in a filament such as

Fig. 94 (above). Black walnut, 1 × 7¾ × 16⅝ in (2.54 × 20 × 42 cm), was cut across the tree so there is growth wood along both edges and the contour of the bark on one. It was selected as the basis for this polyglot fruit-and-vegetable panel, which depicts 63 varieties. Fig. 95 (below). Designs selected from a textbook were sketched on the wood to form a compact group. When the depth of the board was covered at one end, grounding-out was begun, followed by modelling of individual designs. Note that overlaps are left undecided until actual modelling is done, and that carving is not completely laid out and then completely grounded, as the texts instruct. It's more fun this way!

a root, or to slope the tool away. If a section is to be narrower than that, it should be roughed wider, then shaved in finishing, particularly across grain. Very small and delicate filaments such as stems are best cut with the knife. Then, splitting and shattering of thin filaments won't be too much of a problem. Background need not be entirely smooth, but corners should be cleaned out as you go, so the finished work is crisp.

Texturing is largely a matter of V-tool and veiner work, either as lines or scallops. Heavy shaping can be done with the chisels, fine shaping with the knife. I found that a pocketknife—my favorite tool—was unnecessary. Except for veining, designs on the bevelled edge were carved in intaglio entirely with the knife. The peppercorn shapes were "drilled" by rotating a ⅛-in (3.2-mm) half-round gouge. It is important in such work to avoid destroying the edge of the carving, which removes the patina—or in this case, the dark veined surface.

Finish was two coats of sprayed matte varnish to seal the surface, followed by a coat of special walnut color Minwax®, brushed in and wiped off the surfaces in the dark areas, and carefully painted into the background and lines in the light areas to avoid darkening them. This "antiquing" makes the carving appear deeper and sets off the designs. Sandpaper was *not* used, except for a worn piece of very-fine grade rubbed over the top surfaces before varnishing to add a little gloss.

Fig. 96. The rounded contour of the tree perimeter was originally planned to be left in its inner-bark, dark-brown condition. However, condiments were drawn there and whittled out with penknife, through the bark into the growth wood beneath, into a sort of reversed scrimshaw.

CHAPTER XVIII
Likeness of an Unusual Likeness

Color in a Picasso original suggested by texture in a carving

THE PAINTER'S HANDICAP IS THE LACK of a third dimension; on occasion he tries to overcome it by slathering on pigment or using gesso to generate a texture. The sculptor's handicap is lack of color—unless he paints his finished work. This fundamental difference in the two arts becomes important if a woodcarver attempts to reproduce a painting, or vice versa. This is a case in point.

One of my students at Brasstown, North Carolina, David Peters, wanted to reproduce a Picasso painting as a woodcarving. He ultimately selected a detail from "Dora Marr Seated," which had been on the cover of *Time* magazine during the 1980 Picasso show in New York City. The idea was to capture the bold, vivid color of the original with texturing alone.

Wood was walnut, a ¾ × 11 × 12-in (1.9 × 28 × 30-cm) panel, and carving was relatively shallow. The background was textured with a large gouge, while the head itself was trenched around. Various gouge textures were used to suggest the reds, yellows and blues of the original, while smooth, flat planes were created to catch the light and suggest the white. The result was a strong and vivid, easily recognizable likeness. Original finish was two coats of Kiwi® natural shoe polish. This proved to have so high a gloss that it destroyed some of the textural effects, so it was removed with alcohol and replaced by two coats of Deft®.

Fig. 97. A three-dimensional copy of a detail of Picasso's Dora Marr Seated. This is a low-relief carving in walnut, ¾ × 11 × 12 in (1.9 × 28 × 30 cm).

CHAPTER XIX
Twelve Days of Christmas

A familiar carol in a panel

THE IDEA OF REPRESENTING THE POPULAR CAROL "The Twelve Days of Christmas" in symbols on a fir tree was suggested by a 1980 Christmas advertisement. However, the artist apparently hadn't had available the older English versions of the song, or had altered them to suit his plan. Thus, I began some research.

A partridge is a European bird resembling the quail in America, where it is the ruffed grouse in the Northeast and the bobwhite in the South and parts of the West. The turtledove in Europe is *S. turtur*, mostly cinnamon brown; in the United States it is the mourning dove, mostly grey. The three "French" hens were a confusion until I seemed to remember that this was an old name for the guinea hen. The four "colley" birds are blackbirds (not "canary" or "calling" as many Americans sing it).

There were similar problems in selecting the correct kind of pipes for the pipers and drums for the drummers. My selection for wood was Oregon pine. 12 in (30 cm) wide and 2 in (5.1 cm) thick, and I took the background down almost a full inch (2.54 cm) so modelling could be fairly deep. Individual figures and lines, however, were still unclear at any distance, so the tree and figures were painted with oils in bright colors. Background is natural wood color, textured with a flat gouge and spray-varnished with satin finish.

Fig. 98. " The Twelve Days of Christmas, " in pine, 2 × 12 × 19 in (5.1 × 30 × 48 cm), painted with oils.

CHAPTER XX
Carving in Southeast Asia

India, Sri Lanka and Nepal have a long tradition

CARVING IN INDIA, SRI LANKA and Nepal is a tradition. It is also a cottage industry at best, and at worst, a "factory" setup where the factory usually provides relatively little in facilities and acts primarily as a collecting and selling operation. Economies in all three countries are very poor by Western standards, and the men who carve do so strictly for a living; thus, almost everything they make is a tourist item.

In the factories, there may be power saws and sanders—if there is power—and carving is usually done in small areas or particular villages, each place with its own specialized subjects. Tools are limited, often home-made, and worktables are often the floor. Woods are usually what is available locally, though ebony, scarce in Sri Lanka, is carved in Galle—which is not particularly close to the supply. Carvers cut and condition most of their own wood, which is known only by local names, except in one or two larger factories (one in Nepal).

Fig. 99. Miniature contemplative Buddha is Sri Lankan, ebony, and about 4 in (10 cm) tall.

In contrast to the United States, where most carvings are small and 3-D, these people do many relief panels, traditional and modern. The same piece may be available in several different kinds of wood. There are schools where apprentices are taught; I found one up a dirt road in Sigiriya, Sri Lanka, that had perhaps 15 apprentices, mostly boys aged 12 to 20 who went to school in the morning and worked eight hours thereafter. The school had no electricity, so all was hand work, some done after dark by camp lantern.

Most intricate of the carvings are statues of gods and goddesses (mostly Hindu) from all three countries, and the masks from Sri Lanka. Figures of Buddha are particularly common in Sri Lanka, a largely Buddhist country, and are quite cheap. Carvers seem unconcerned about wood hardness, because all use chisels and mallets—the latter usually a shaped club. Some mahogany is carved, usually for furniture, and most in-the-round pieces are ebony, because that sells better to tourists. Exceptions are the larger panels, often in either hard or soft lighter-colored woods, and masks, which are made in nux vomica, a wood about as soft as balsa, with poisonous fruit processed in pharmaceuticals. Some of the very intricate work, such as the goddess in figure 100, is also done in lighter-colored hardwoods.

Fig. 100. These small household gods are Zogini (left) from Nepal, 7 in (18 cm) tall, and Lakshmi (goddess), 6 in (15 cm) tall, from India. Both are carved in-the-round of single blocks, then mounted on half-round bases; the Zogini, however, is mounted against a separately carved background, while the Lakshmi has a one-piece carved back and aura. Zogini, in a wood called adinacopifolia, is more intricate than the Indian figure, though it was cheaper by far, because the Indian figure was in a "tourist trap" and carved in a scarce sandalwood with a darker base, while I got the Nepalese one at a "factory."

Fig. 101 (right). Carver starting a lion in a Galle, Sri Lanka, factory. His tools are carpenter's chisels with homemade handles, and his mallet is a club.

Fig. 102 (below). Lion, about 5½ × 8½ in (14 × 22 cm), was carved in a very heavy and hard red wood by a 14-year-old apprentice at Sigiriya, Sri Lanka. It has inserted tongue, and toenails and teeth of elephant bone in lieu of scarce and expensive ivory.

Fig. 103 (left). Pingo porter 10 in (25 cm) tall, in ebony, wears a long loin clout and turban. He is carrying fish to market in the panniers (fish carved on top). This is standard carrying technique in Sri Lanka.

Fig. 104 (right). Farmer, in breech clout and turban, carries a separate mattock, made in two pieces and inserted, as well as a small bag of food. This is also ebony, 10 in (25 cm) tall, and carved in Galle.

Fig. 105 (below). Fishermen in Hikkaduwa, on the south coast of Sri Lanka, thrust poles into the shallows at good fishing spots. They move from one to the other as the tide changes, carrying with them the cross-arm they sit on above waterlevel. This ebony carving is about 10 in (25 cm) tall and one piece, except for the pole and fish. Fig. 106 (right). The Bonkura horse is made in various materials and sizes in northern India; it is a stylization of an old-time warrior's horse according to one version of the story and a trader's horse according to another.

Fig. 107 (right). Ancient queen of Sri Lanka holds a lotus in each hand. Note slanted eyes, elaborate hairdo and low-slung sari. The ebony figure is about 10 in (25 cm) tall, with copper earrings.

CHAPTER XXI

Nuts, Pits and Gourds

Common fruits yield unusual carvings in many lands

VARIOUS NUTS ARE CARVED ALL OVER the world, because they provide a basic shape and a woody texture. One of the first things I learned to carve was a peach pit, but it was many years later that I realized it was also possible to carve plum and apricot pits, coconut shell and hard-shelled gourds. In recent years, I have also seen carved avocado pits (Israel), olive pits (China), nutmeg and walnut shell (Mexico), hickory nuts and butternuts (USA) and many kinds of hard seeds used for beads, particularly in the Pacific Islands.

Perhaps the most unusual carved nuts come from an area in Ecuador. They are from a palm, the tagua, which grows in Ecuador and Colombia. These nuts are slightly smaller and flatter than hen's eggs, with brown skins and hard white meat—so hard, in fact, that it is called vegetable ivory and even carves like the real thing. Designs range from pipes to chess sets and elaborate assemblies such as the skeleton in figure 114. The nut is not available commercially, except as carved, as nearly as I can discover—a pity—but the designs can be done in holly or other dense woods.

My general experience with carving nuts, pits and gourds has shown all of them to be brittle and hard. Chips tend to break away rather than cut, and carving is a slow process that requires frequent resharpening of tools. But finished pieces will take a good finish and can usually be stained or painted. The carved gourds of Peru are particularly noted for intricacy of detail in the shallow carved and painted surfaces, usually in brown and black only. The tagua nuts are often in full color, painted expertly with oils, and the heads are accurate likenesses. The 2-in (5.1-cm) long "olive" pits that formerly came from China were far more intricate, however—I had one carved as a sampan, with window shutters that actually opened and showed images behind them, all from a shell wall under ⅛ in (3.2 mm) thick! These were undoubtedly the work of ivory carvers.

Fig. 108. This primitive lathe, assembled from scrap wood and iron by a Mexican Indian, is used to turn and bore hard seeds for necklaces. He rotates the spindle with a bow in his right hand, and guides a tool with his left. The work is held between centers by a heavy spring between the wood uprights. Later, he uses a drill made from a nail to bore the center hole.

Work like this is almost unknown to Americans, even tourists, because these pieces are produced in small quantities and are not generally available in tourist shops. The assembly of parts made from separate nuts or other materials is also very unusual. In Mexico, walnut and coconut-shell segments are assembled into various animals as decorative units, some of which can be opened to reveal scenes assembled from bits of paper and wood, painted. In Chile I found about ten varieties of animal shapes glued together from sections of peach pits. Such work would not be attempted in the United States because it would not repay the time and effort involved. I have, however, seen several elaborate peach-pit carvings, one a caricature of Richard Nixon when he was president. And pendants and buttons sawed from hickory nuts have been around for years. Start with them or with peach or nectarine pits, which are readily available. A knife is really all the equipment you need for peach-pit carving, plus a little imagination to see what the surface convolutions suggest.

Fig. 109 (left). Peach-pit assemblies from Chile involve at least ten shapes of familiar animals and birds. Here are a rabbit and a swan, of pieces glued together and tinted.

Figs. 110–111 (right and below). Gourds are carved in various Latin-American countries, but the most elaborate come from Peru. Carving is surface scratching, like scrimshaw, but deeper and done in browns and blacks. This one, with a girl's head, is about 7 in (18 cm) tall.

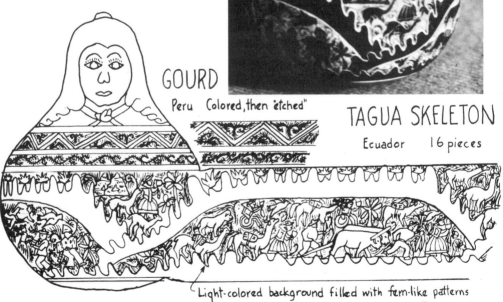

GOURD

Peru Colored, then "etched"

TAGUA SKELETON

Ecuador 16 pieces

Light-colored background filled with fern-like patterns

Figs. 112–113 (right and below). This carved gourd, about 10 in (25 cm) tall, includes people and animals in a sort of stream-of-consciousness design, as in figures 110–111. Only the decorative bands are reminiscent of the old-style decorated gourds and require some layout. A similar technique can be applied to any surface.

Center of base

TRADITIONAL GOURD MOTIFS & TREATMENT

Glossy surface is cut or marked & ink rubbed in, as in scrimshaw.
About ¾ of the major design band is sketched, including
one panel (bull baiting) & various fiesta booths, musicians &
dancers. Foliage scrolls, palm trees & llamas fill interim areas.
Designs are fitted in haphazardly, except on neck & base.

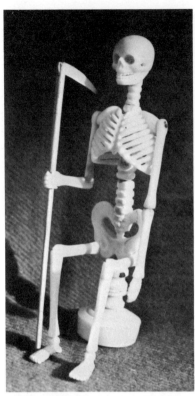

Fig. 114 (left). Tagua-nut skeleton from Ecuador is an assembly of 16 pieces, including a turned base. The scythe blade is also tagua, the handle a wood dowel. The carving, about 8 in (20 cm) tall, is made for the Day of the Dead, November 1, like the American Halloween the night before.

Fig. 115 (below). Miscellaneous small tagua-nut carvings include a pipe, a chess knight, and a head of Atahualpa, last Inca emperor. The miniature head is of Bolivar, cut on a plum pit, painted with oils and mounted on a stickpin!

Fig. 116 (above). Heads of three popes, two plain and one tinted, are typical of the profiles carved by Indians in the mountain village of Riobamba, north of Quito.

Figs. 117–118 (above and below). Older tagua carvings tended to be unpainted, as shown by these examples. Two of the five are heads of Jesus and two are Atahualpa, last Inca emperor. The fifth, at right, is a Spaniard. Below are four Indian profiles, two skulls and a head of Columbus. Note that two of the heads are mounted on turned pedestals, also of tagua.

Figs. 119–120 (above and below). Of these two groups of carved taguas from Ecuador, the above includes profiles of Cervantes, Colorado Indians (male and female), an unusual in-the-round head of Rumiñahi, last Inca commander, and a profile of him with Atahualpa, his emperor. Below are Generals Bolívar and Sucre, both folk heroes, and a pair of Otavaleños—an Ecuadorean tribe that has a distinct, old-fashioned-grandee dress and appearance.

Fig. 121 (above). These five Tagua heads again include one in-the-round, the head of a Colorado Indian in dress paint. His hair is daubed with bright red clay. Profiles include another Indian and a Black, as well as two former presidents of Ecuador. Fig. 122 (below). Tagua-carving is very commercial in Colombia; these are typical present-day figures, largely lathe-turned. The girl has hair of braided thread, yellow insulated-copper-wire arms and legs of bare copper wire. The central god figure has been bored to hold salt. There is some carving, but most decoration is painted in bright colors.

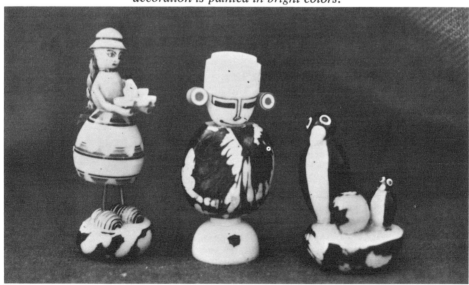

CHAPTER XXII
You Can Carve Thick Bark

Figures, scenes—even patterns for metal-casting

ONE UNFORTUNATE RESULT OF OUR URBAN civilization, and of the fact that most carvers these days begin with a dressed piece of kiln-dried lumber, is the infrequency of an old craft, the carving of bark. It is still done by Indians in Mexico, and I also found it in Nebraska among a group of carvers who work from air-dried logs.

The essential here is a tree that produces a fairly thick bark, such as the catalpa, black cottonwood or ponderosa pine. There are also harder and denser barks, like that of the pochote in Mexico, dense enough to use as patterns for casting precious metals or show a village façade in miniature. I first encountered such work many years ago in Mexico, and found the carving of ponderosa pine bark more recently there.

Fig. 123. At left is a profile, in the middle the Pope wearing a fan-dancer head-dress, as he did during part of his visit to Mexico, and at right a frontal face. All were carved in pine bark by the author in 1979, during a Mexican visit.

Fig. 124 (above). Pochote-bark segments as I cut them from a tree with a machete. Note that they resemble miniature mountains or cliffs, thus, a village can be depicted rather easily. Fig. 125 (right). Single figure in bark is a peon, with an owl overhead. Also by the author.

Fig. 126 (right). Miniature totem pole about 6 in (15 cm) high, carved in black cottonwood bark by James M. Ward in the mid-Seventies. Fig. 127 (below). A plaque with five profiles, a Madonna and Child and a lion's head, all carved in pine bark by the author. Each carving took under an hour and is about 7 in (18 cm).

Ponderosa is carved by the Tarahumara Indians, a primitive tribe living in the state of Chihuahua, Mexico, whose idea of sport includes running down a deer for food. Their pine carvings are crude, though they do make quite good guitars and violins! I got some of the bark and found I could make a fairly complete carving in 20 minutes or a half hour because the bark is so soft. It is laminated and quite brittle, but is more satisfactory for an exercise wood than balsa, for example, and far less expensive because it's free. Catalpa bark is similar, but pochote is dense, dark red with a greyed exterior, and is not at all brittle nor noticeably laminar when carved. Also, it tends to be in "domes" rather than strips, and has an inherent design that frames a carving.

Bark can be finished with sprayed matte or satin varnish to increase surface strength and combat the tendency to crumble. Nebraska carvers, who cut faces in the solid wood of a slab beneath catalpa bark, use a heavy and shiny multi-coat, plastic-based finish to contrast with the rough bark exterior.

Fig. 128 (left). Female figure, with headdress, and triple god faces carved in ponderosa-pine bark by a Tarahumara woman, about 1979. The taller figure is 13 in (33 cm) long.

Fig. 129 (right). Indian figure with shoulder bag and separate hat, about 6 in (15 cm) tall, and a god pendant, both in pine bark. The pendant is carried on a necklace made of whittled-willow beads, again by a Tarahumara woman.

Fig. 130 (left). Somewhat more ambitious doll resembling Buffalo Bill, about 8 in (20 cm) tall. Body and head are one piece, but the hat is glued on over hair taken from a horsetail. Moustache and beard are grey horsehair as well. A good primitive!

CHAPTER XXIII
Bone Is Cheaper Than Ivory

And it carves well, too

ANIMAL-BONE CARVING IS RELATIVELY little known in the United States, although it has been done for centuries by primitive peoples elsewhere in the world. The Balinese are particularly adept at it, carving cow shoulder and leg bones into intricate, usually Hindu, designs. Other South Pacific peoples have carved bone—some of it human, regrettably. Mexicans in and around Guanajuato make a variety of bone carvings from cow bone, ranging from statuettes to small finger rings and pins. It is likely that American carvers will be doing more carving of bone as the controls on ivory increase, or the supply itself diminishes because the animals that provide it are hunted to extinction. Even the Eskimos in Alaska, who still have access to walrus tusk (at inflated prices), are carving whalebone on occasion.

Figs. 131–133 (above and on facing page). A man's bracelet (wood with bone appliques), a pin and a carved eagle, all in buffalo bone by Ruth T. Brunstetter, Hyde Park, New York. Mrs. Brunstetter, an artist, took up the mounting of animal skeletons some years back, and now has an extensive collection. This bone is from a friend who has a small buffalo herd in New York State.

Such bone as I have carved—cow and sheep—is harder than most woods but softer than ivory. It can be whittled with a knife, or carved with chisels if it can be held (beware of hand-holding when you use chisels—they may slip). Bone is also more open-grained than ivory and more brittle, so it is a natural candidate for rasps and files and power grinders. It can be polished like ivory, and painted or tinted.

Fig. 132.

Fig. 133.

CHAPTER XXIV
Carve Stone and Shell

It's easier than it looks

MANY KINDS OF STONE HAVE BEEN CARVED by man, ranging from the soft ones such as soapstone, onyx and alabaster through harder ones such as pipestone, jade, marble and granite on to very hard ones that include emerald, ruby and sapphire. The soft stones can be carved or whittled like wood with a pocketknife or simple woodcarving chisels (except that edge angle should be increased), while the hardest can be cut only with diamond. And many peoples have done the carving, from the scratch drawings of primitive man in Europe to present-day sculpture. Indian tribes in the Americas have done their share, including the Inca, the Cherokee and various tribes in Minnesota and along the Northwest Coast from Washington through British Columbia to Alaska. Eskimos have carved soapstone and greenstone as well, using primitive tools of harder stone until we brought them steel ones. The Polynesians, Chinese, Japanese and Italians are *still* expert stone carvers.

I have whittled soapstone, pipestone and onyx. It is a slow process involving frequent sharpening of the knife. Pipestone, incidentally, is one of a variety of stones that are softer when first mined and harden with exposure to air. It is dense and fine-grained, and will support a great amount of detail. Pipestone is mined in Minnesota, and legend has it that all tribes went there for it before the white man came. The mines are still considered sacred areas and only Indians may mine the stone.

The Turks seem to have a practical monopoly on another and quite different pipe mineral, meerschaum, because they control its source—Asia Minor. It is anhydrous magnesium silicate, soft, porous, fine-grained and clay-like, but light enough to float in water, and is carved into the finest and most expensive pipes and cigarholders in the world.

Shell is an animal product rather than a mineral, but it carves quite similarly and also has a similar brittleness and lamination. I am speaking primarily of marine shells, though turtle shell has been carved for centuries as well. The latter is comparatively soft, and tends to make the tool edge stick, as do plastics. Sea turtles, however, are now an endangered species, and even land turtles are becoming much less common, so there is little likelihood of shell being carved in the future. Of the various kinds of turtle shell, that from sea turtles is heavier and more attractive, and can be formed and separated into layers as well as carved.

In India and Africa, small triton and other shells are carved and etched with surface designs. Italy is the great Western source of carved shell, particularly the cameo, which is carved in one kind of shell that has a lining lighter than the outer layers so that a carved head or other figure can be set out against an integral background. Italians also carve figures from the core of the conch shell. Maori tribesmen, on the other hand, used the paua shell to decorate their woodcarvings, but did not carve it. This shell is like abalone, which the American Indians of the Northwest incorporated into their carvings in similar fashion, by setting pieces into sockets and holding them with a natural glue. In Mexico, extremely elaborate mosaics are produced by setting shaped bits of shell into a black composition that hardens and can then be polished. Here, the wood acts primarily as a frame.

Figs. 134–135 (above and right). Two views of a triangular pipestone fragment, about 1 × 2 × 2½ in (2.54 × 5.1 × 6.4 cm) and carved by Robert Reed, a Cherokee, which includes 22 separate pictures. Above can be seen an Indian head and a skull with a snake, while the view at right includes a partial human head, hawk and quail heads and a bear. Actual size of the Indian head in figure 134 is the same as on an old penny.

Figs. 136–137 (above and upper right). Soapstone and pipestone pieces by Charlie Reed, a Cherokee. The pipestone piece above is only 1 in (2.54 cm) long but contains nine units, in which can be seen a large frog swallowing a human head with a smaller frog atop it. The soapstone piece at upper right is 1½ in (3.8 cm) wide and has a number of figures. Shown here is a face and body with upraised arm, which on the back is also the thumb of a hand. Also shown are a bird head, a turtle and a crab-like figure along the bottom.

Fig. 138 (right). Simple red pipestone carving by S. Toomi, a Cherokee, is about 2 in (5.1 cm) long and shows an Indian girl bathing beneath a waterfall.

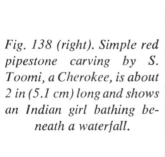

106

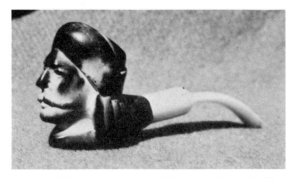

Figs. 139–141 (above, right and below). Two Turkish meerschaum pipes purchased in Jerusalem. The white head of the chieftain at right is much more detailed, and the meerschaum is much higher grade, so it cost five times what the other one did.

Fig. 140.

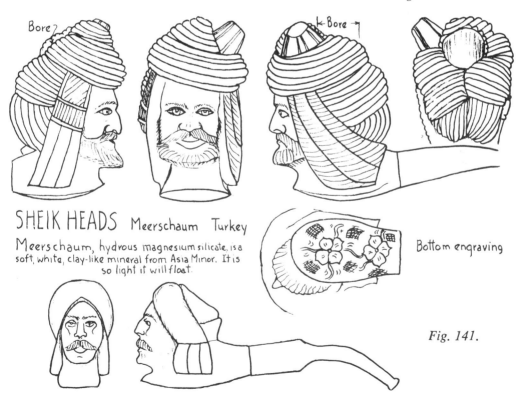

Bore?

←Bore→

SHEIK HEADS Meerschaum Turkey

Meerschaum, hydrous magnesium silicate, is a soft, white, clay-like mineral from Asia Minor. It is so light it will float.

Bottom engraving

Fig. 141.

107

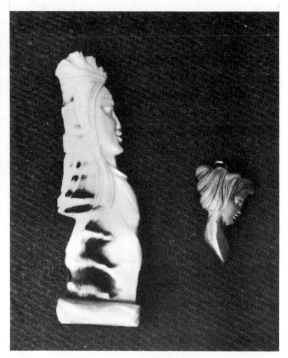

Fig. 142 (above). Cameo shell with a finished cameo ready to be cut out. Fig. 143 (right). Two shell figures from Italy. The larger appears to be the core of a conch shell; the small head of a girl is from a cameo-shell core.

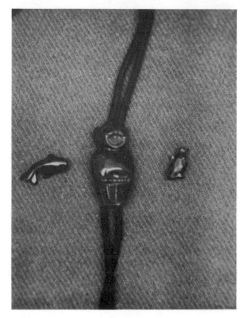

Fig. 144 (above). Pendant and cross from Mexico, with shell fragments set in a black base and polished. Wood in pieces like this is primarily a backing. Fragments are cut with coping saw and files. Fig. 145 (right). Alaskan jadeite whale and Billiken bolo slide. The Billiken has a gold nugget in his navel; rubbing it is supposed to bring good luck.

The small bird at right is of wood.

Figs. 146–147 (above and below). One tribe of Indians north of Lima, Peru, carves a brilliant soft white stone like soapstone, called huamonga. The usual product is a Nativity scene, which may be single pieces perhaps ¾ in (19 mm) high, the Holy Family mounted in a small painted wooden box or an elaborate Nativity with a background and base carved from soapstone of the familiar variety—striated grey.

Figs. 148–149 (left and below). Here are two views of a stone carved by John Julius Wilnoty, top Cherokee stone carver. View at left shows a hawk and grinning mask, while below can be seen a face and the coils of a stylized snake. The stone is roughly 2 in (5.1 cm) square.

Figs. 150–151 (above and below). Tiny fish, frogs, a cat and other pieces carved from semi-precious stones by Indians in Brazil. The largest is less than an inch (2.54 cm) long.

Fig. 152 (above). Two birds and a fish carved from semi-precious stones by Indians in Mexico. The central bird is about ⅝ in (16 mm) long; the fish at right is a fire opal.

Fig. 153 (right). Tiny onyx fruits and vegetables are an unusual Indian product near Puebla, Mexico. Here are bananas, pineapple, sugar cane, avocado, apple, pepper and other examples, shown full size. They are tinted with dyes.

Fig. 154 (left). This double walrus head is in soapstone, with walrus-ivory tusks. It was carved in Alaska back in the Fifties.

CHAPTER XXV
Horn Can Be Carved and Formed

It is in Northwestern America, Chile, Mexico and India

CARVING AND SHAPING ANIMAL HORN is another craft that approaches wood-carving, and one that has been practiced in many countries. In earlier books, I described birds shaped from horn that I discovered in the USSR, Indochina, Mexico and Bali. More recently, I have found carved cowhorns in Chile, and formed and carved ones—the most elaborate I've seen—in India. The Indian ones also appear to be dyed and resemble turtle shell, or may be a much darker horn.

Pieces from Chile include horns with surface-carved scenes, horns carved in-the-round and assemblies—usually a lady with a basket. As nearly as I can discover, the horn is boiled or otherwise heated, then carved while hot; it is brittle when cold and dry. Heat was obviously involved in the Indian shaped pieces, such as the lion, with decoration applied later by scratching so that the torn surface of the cut shows almost white against the darker horn. In Mexico and India, small in-the-round pieces like pendants are carved from the thicker horn at the tip. The American Northwest Coast Indians shaped mountain-sheep horn into spoons, some with elaborately carved handles. It's enjoyable—if you can find the horn.

Fig. 155. Carved and shaped horn lion is typical of fine Indian work in this specialized field. It is about 10 in (25 cm) long and dark brown, with lighter scratched decoration.

Fig. 156 (above). Girl figure with basket made from separate cow-horn tip, and horn showing house, fence and mountain, both from Patagonian Chile. Fig. 157 (below). Girl figures, 8 and 12 in (20 and 30 cm), carved from cow horn in Chile.

Figs. 158–159 (right and below). Devil head carved from horn in Patagonia, Chile. It has a chain for hanging.

Fig. 159.

CHAPTER XXVI

Ivory Carving – an Ancient Art

As a CARVING MATERIAL AND OBJECT OF veneration, ivory dates back to the Paleolithic Era 15,000 years ago. It has been carved by men all over the world, and from such diverse sources as elephant, walrus, hippo, rhino and whale, to say nothing of exhumed mastodon and mammoth. It is probably the finest carving material for miniatures, but all of its sources are now endangered species. Some of the history of this material is given in Chapter 19 of *Carving Wooden Animals* (Sterling, 1980).

Ivory is essentially like human teeth. Thus, it has a hard surface called the enamel, a whiter, softer area under that called the dentine, and finally a core of even softer material that looks like clotted, discolored cheese pressed solid. Usual practice is to grind or chip off the enamel layer and carve the dentine; this eliminates surface defects and discoloration while making carving easier. I have, however, carved walrus-tusk enamel layers with a pocketknife and small wood chisels. It is slow, difficult carving, and frequent sharpening is necessary. Ivory can be sawed and rasped easily, which is the way much of the very elaborate Chinese pierced carving is done.

Ivory has very little grain, but it does tend to laminate and dry out as it ages. Thus, I was able to make carvings of a polar bear and puffins from layers of dentine cut loose from a tusk core, and use the remainder as a background. Elephant ivory in large chunks is also extremely sensitive to heat. A high-intensity lamp close by, sudden changes of temperature or too much concentration with power burr, grinder or buffer may cause cracking. And because ivory is animal in origin, carving with power tools may create a smell like that of burning bones—decidedly unpleasant. But power carving is now the common approach by professionals, from Alaskan Eskimos to Germans, whenever power and power tools are available.

American scrimshaw carvers, of which there are a great many, still work largely by hand, because scrimshanding is basically a scratching process. Sailors did it with a nail set into a piece of dowel and filled the scratches with smoke or paint, then sanded the surface to remove excess coloring.

Chinese carvers still use tea and smoke to tint their work, and I have an Indian piece made recently that I think was antiqued that way.

Old ivory gradually turns yellow and tends to develop surface cracks. I have found that I can antique an ivory carving with stain in the same way I would one in wood, by coating the surface and promptly wiping off the excess. The stain stays in the cracks, and should not be too dark. Polishing should be a careful operation because any sanding tends to blur the sharp edges of the carving and make them less visible by reducing the strong edge shadows. Polishing with something like jewelers rouge or with paste silver polish, which Alaska Eskimos use, does the least damage.

If you want to try ivory carving, hunt up some old piano keys, cue balls or other large old pieces. You can make many smaller pieces from each. Or you may, as I did, find a friend who has a spare old walrus tusk or chunk of ivory from China. It's fun and very rewarding!

Fig. 160. This walrus tusk, about 15 in (38 cm) long, was given to me by a friend for experimentation. I carved 14 animals on it with pocketknife, hook knife, veiner and V-tool, cutting through the dentine in each case because I didn't know it should be taken off initially.

Drilled hole lengthwise

Bow view

Actual size

Integral hinged double doors open to show man inside!

Oars & rudder assumed

Separate wood base

SAMPAN Old China Ivory

Figs. 161–162 (above and below). Chinese ivory carvings tend to be extremely detailed. This is a complete sampan, with a detailed structure and even passengers. It is about 4 in (10 cm) long, with ¼-in (6.4-mm) shutters that open and close!

Figs. 163–164 (right and below). From India come these two recent pieces. At right is a goddess carved from scrap, and below, an elephant being attacked by a bird. Pieces like this have now become costly, even in India.

Fig. 165 (above). Polar bear and puffins mounted on the butts of an old walrus tusk, which was laminated and, thus, permitted a front section to be sawed out. The blackish porous central mound is where the blood vessels meet the solid tusk; the thin upper area meets the walrus' upper jaw. Puffins are painted with oils to proper colors. Fig. 166 (below). Two cormorant carvings by Alaskan Eskimos. The taller one is mastodon ivory, and the smaller ones are from King Island and mounted on a whale vertebra.

Fig. 167 (right). Eagle pendant and earrings for the U.S. Bicentennial (1976)—again, whittled.

Fig. 168 (left). Flying goose, from a laminate of walrus tusk 3 in (7.6 cm) long, is mounted on music wire inserted into a California-ironwood base. The cattail at the base of the wire is also walrus ivory.

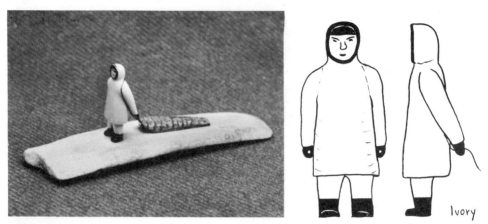

Figs. 169–170 (above, left to right). From St. Lawrence Island, Alaska, comes this ivory assembly, with a 2-in (5.1-cm) Eskimo drawing a red-tinted sledge of walrus meat. Both are mounted on a piece of fossil ivory 6 in (15 cm) long.

Fig. 171. The Japanese have long produced netsuke—small pieces of wood or ivory once used to pull the drawcords on purses men carried in their kimono sashes. Though many are now made primarily for well-heeled American collectors, they are delightful miniature in-the-round subjects. These are ivory.

Fig. 172 (right). Musk ox and 2-in (5.1-cm) duck were blanks sawed out by an Eskimo who deserted them for the pipeline. I found the blanks in an Anchorage shop and whittled them on the way home.

Fig. 173 (left). Billikens 2¾ and 2 in (7 and 5.1 cm). These good-luck charms are walrus-tusk tips from Skagway, Alaska.

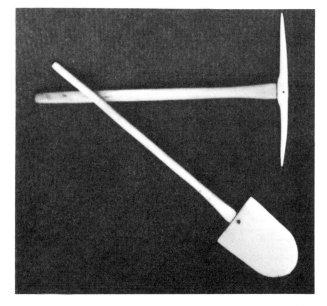

Fig. 174 (right). Utilitarian walrus-ivory antiques comprise a miner's pick and shovel carved about 1910 in Alaska and brought around the Horn. Each is about 7 in (18 cm) long.

APPENDIX I
Some Notes on Sharpening

NOWADAYS, MOST REPUTABLE SOURCES of tools sell them sharpened. The rough grinding of a forged tool requires a wheel, and if not properly done will result in a burned or distorted edge. Also, many carvers now maintain the edge on tools by buffing or power sanding, which is faster and much easier than the hand operation. (One sort of power-sharpening setup is shown in *Capturing Personality in Woodcarving*, Sterling, 1981.)

Traditionally, sharpening consisted of four separate steps: grinding, whetting, honing and stropping. Grinding is a rough operation required only initially or if a tool is broken or chipped. Whetting and honing are hand operations done on progressively finer-grained stones. Whetting is done on *Washita*, a yellowish or greyish natural stone, honing on *Arkansas*, a stone that is white, very hard and uniform. Arkansas is also the stone used in "slips," which are small stones shaped with a taper, vee or curve to fit inside a tool edge and clean away any burr or feather edge generated by coarser sharpening. (There are now manufactured stones for these operations as well.) Stropping is done as a barber does on a straight razor—with a piece of leather belt, often mounted on a wood paddle so that there is a coarse leather surface impregnated with abrasive and oil on one side, smooth leather with just oil on the other.

In normal carving, particularly with soft woods, the strop supplemented occasionally by the hone will keep an edge razor-sharp. But this degree of sharpness may be too much for heavy carving, particularly of hard materials such as stone or shell, where a blunter tool will hold its edge longer. Even when carving very hard woods such as ebony and cocobola, as well as ivory, pipestone, bone and shell, the actual included angle of the tool edge can be reduced as well, particularly if the tools used are a mallet and chisels.

There are a number of tricks to sharpening. Several are shown in figures 175 and 176. In addition, makers of stones, such as Norton, frequently provide detailed instructions.

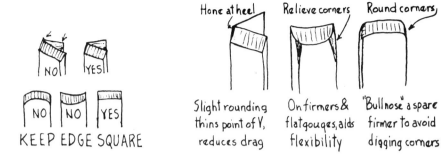

NO | YES

NO | NO | YES

KEEP EDGE SQUARE

Hone at heel — Slight rounding thins point of V, reduces drag

Relieve corners — On firmers & flat gouges, aids flexibility

Round corners — "Bullnose" a spare firmer to avoid digging corners

Fig. 175.

INNER BEVEL on GOUGE
After whetting, hone a <u>very</u> slight bevel on inner face to avoid digging in & to lengthen edge life.

STONING A FIRMER — & A GOUGE
<u>Push</u> edge-first (<u>Pull</u> on strop)   Roll & pull along

Fig. 176.

APPENDIX II
Two Ways to Change Pattern Size

THE EASIEST WAY TO CHANGE THE SIZE of an available photo, sketch or other pattern is to have it photostated or rephotographed to the desired size. A similar method is to take a photograph of the subject and then project the negative to the right size. There are also pantographs and proportioning dividers, which work reasonably well if you can arrive at an even multiple for enlargement or reduction.

Failing any of the above, there are two familiar methods to change the size of a pattern. One is to draw a grid on a piece of transparent paper or plastic that can be laid over the source material. Usually, ⅛-in (3.2-mm) spacing between lines is close enough. It is also possible to use graph paper over a photo or sketch if you can get a light source behind it; I do this by holding paper and photo or sketch against a windowpane facing the sun. Then you make a matching grid with lines spaced for the desired enlargement. Example: If you're doubling size, line spacing is ¼ in (6.4 mm); if you're tripling, it's ⅜ in (9.6 mm); if you're going to 1½ size, it's ³⁄₁₆ in (4.8 mm) and so on. Then the design is copied from one grid to the other, square-by-square.

I find that I can get confused and lost copying square-by-square, and I draw reasonably well. Thus, I use the point-to-point method. In this case, you draw or apply a base and a side line to the source material, and put a corresponding pair of reference lines on the wood or copy paper. Then you measure from the reference lines to prominent points on the original, multiply resulting measurements by the necessary amount and measure off these spaces on the copy. Thus, if a side measurement to a point is 1¼ in (3.2 cm) and a vertical measurement is 1½ in (3.8 cm), and you're doubling size. you lay out 2½ in (6.4 cm) from the side and 3 in (7.6 cm) up from the base line on the copy. When you have located a sufficient number of reference points, you sketch in the desired outline just as the kids follow the numbers in the Sunday comic section.

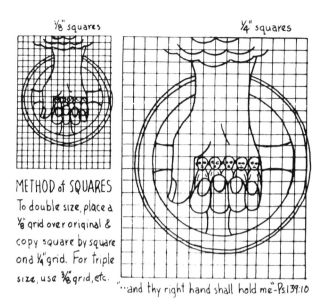

Fig. 177.

METHOD of SQUARES
To double size, place a ⅛" grid over original & copy square by square ond ¼" grid. For triple size, use ⅜" grid, etc.

"...and thy right hand shall hold me"-Ps.139:10

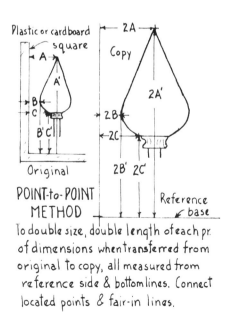

Plastic or cardboard square

Copy

Original

Reference base

Fig. 178.

POINT-to-POINT METHOD
To double size, double length of each pr. of dimensions when transferred from original to copy, all measured from reference side & bottom lines. Connect located points & fair-in lines.

Index